TEACHER'S PET PUBLICATIONS

LITPLAN TEACHER PACK
for
The Red Badge of Courage
based on the book by
Stephen Crane

Written by
Mary B. Collins

© 1996 Teacher's Pet Publications
All Rights Reserved

This **LitPlan** for Stephen Crane's
The Red Badge of Courage
has been brought to you by Teacher's Pet Publications, Inc.

Copyright Teacher's Pet Publications 1996
11504 Hammock Point
Berlin MD 21811

Only the student materials in this unit plan
such as worksheets, study questions, assignment sheets, and tests
may be reproduced multiple times for use in the purchaser's classroom.

For any additional copyright questions,
contact Teacher's Pet Publications.

www.tpet.com

TABLE OF CONTENTS - *The Red Badge of Courage*

Introduction	5
Unit Objectives	7
Reading Assignment Sheet	8
Unit Outline	9
Study Questions (Short Answer)	13
Quiz/Study Questions (Multiple Choice)	22
Pre-reading Vocabulary Worksheets	37
Lesson One (Introductory Lesson)	55
Nonfiction Assignment Sheet	57
Oral Reading Evaluation Form	59
Writing Assignment 1	63
Writing Assignment 2	74
Writing Assignment 3	77
Writing Evaluation Form	71
Vocabulary Review Activities	65
Extra Writing Assignments/Discussion ?s	69
Unit Review Activities	79
Unit Tests	83
Unit Resource Materials	111
Vocabulary Resource Materials	125

A FEW NOTES ABOUT THE AUTHOR
STEPHEN CRANE

CRANE, Stephen (1871-1900). A novelist, poet, and short-story writer, Stephen Crane is considered one of the six most outstanding American novelists and short-story writers of the 19th century. He is regarded as a pioneer of social and psychological realism in American literature.

Crane was born in Newark, N.J., on Nov. 1, 1871, into a family in which there were many Methodist ministers. He rebelled in many ways against the family's morality, but his writings were to reflect his religious background. His schooling was sporadic; nonetheless he read all of the 19th-century English writers and the Greek and Roman classics.

Crane worked as a free-lance writer in New York City in the early 1890s, and there he wrote 'Maggie: a Girl of the Streets', first published in 1893. The novel displayed a realism that set the literary trend of the following generation. He then wrote 'Red Badge of Courage' (1895), which he intended to be "a psychological portrayal of fear." Crane also achieved mastery of the short story. His volumes of them include 'The Little Regiment, and Other Episodes of the American Civil War' (1896) and 'The Open Boat, and Other Tales of Adventure' (1898).

Crane's poetry was of a rhymeless, rhythmic, free-form style. He also did journalistic reporting in Greece and Cuba. Crane died on June 5, 1900, in Badenweiler, Germany, of tuberculosis, compounded by a recurring malaria fever he had contracted in Cuba while reporting on the Spanish-American War.

-- Courtesy of Compton's Learning Company

INTRODUCTION

This unit has been designed to develop students' reading, writing, thinking, and language skills through exercises and activities related to *The Red Badge of Courage* by Stephen Crane. It includes twenty lessons, supported by extra resource materials.

The **introductory lesson** introduces students to one main idea of the novel through a visual activity and discussion of students' relevant personal experiences. Following the introductory activity, students are given a transition to explain how the activity relates to the book they are about to read. Following the transition, students are given the materials they will be using during the unit. At the end of the lesson, students begin the pre-reading work for the first reading assignment.

The **reading assignments** are approximately fifteen pages each; some are a little shorter while others are a little longer. Students have approximately 15 minutes of pre-reading work to do prior to each reading assignment. This pre-reading work involves reviewing the study questions for the assignment and doing some vocabulary work for 8 to 10 vocabulary words they will encounter in their reading.

The **study guide questions** are fact-based questions; students can find the answers to these questions right in the text. These questions come in two formats: short answer required or multiple choice. The best use of these materials is probably to use the short answer version of the questions as study guides for students (since answers will be more complete), and to use the multiple choice version for occasional quizzes. It might be a good idea to make transparencies of your answer keys for the overhead projector.

The **vocabulary work** is intended to enrich students' vocabularies as well as to aid in the students' understanding of the book. Prior to each reading assignment, students will complete a two-part worksheet for approximately 8 to 10 vocabulary words in the upcoming reading assignment. Part I focuses on students' use of general knowledge and contextual clues by giving the sentence in which the word appears in the text. Students are then to write down what they think the words mean based on the words' usage. Part II nails down the definitions of the words by giving students dictionary definitions of the words and having students match the words to the correct definitions based on the words' contextual usage. Students should then have an understanding of the words when they meet them in the text.

After each reading assignment, students will go back and formulate answers for the study guide questions. Discussion of these questions serves as a **review** of the most important events and ideas presented in the reading assignments.

After students complete reading the work, there is a **vocabulary review** lesson which pulls together all of the fragmented vocabulary lists for the reading assignments and gives students a review of all of the words they have studied.

Following the vocabulary review, a lesson is devoted to the **extra discussion questions/writing assignments**. These questions focus on interpretation, critical analysis and personal response, employing a variety of thinking skills and adding to the students' understanding of the novel.

The **group activity** which follows the discussion questions has students working in small and large groups to prepare a case either defending or prosecuting Henry for desertion. Students first get together in small groups to review the facts of the case (the text) and prepare their arguments. Then they get together in larger groups (one defense and one prosecution) to actually prepare the case and prepare their witnesses. When the students have completed preparing their cases, an actual mini-trial is held to determine Henry's guilt or innocence.

There are three **writing assignments** in this unit, each with the purpose of informing, persuading, or having students express personal opinions. The first assignment is to express personal opinions: students take a realistic look at how they think they would perform in combat. The second assignment is to persuade: following the mini-trial, students create a written composition in which they argue for or against Henry's conviction. The third assignment is to inform: students research and report about conflicts/wars which are happening in the present day.

Writing Assignment #3 is done in conjunction with a **nonfiction reading assignment**. Students are required to read articles about conflicts/wars which are going on in our world today. After reading their nonfiction pieces, students give **oral presentations** followed by Writing Assignment #3. This not only exposes all students to a wealth of information, it also gives students the opportunity to practice **public speaking**.

The **review lesson** pulls together all of the aspects of the unit. The teacher is given four or five choices of activities or games to use which all serve the same basic function of reviewing all of the information presented in the unit.

The **unit test** comes in two formats: short answer or multiple choice. As a convenience, two different tests for each format have been included. Also there is an advanced unit test which is mostly composition.

There are additional **support materials** included with this unit. The **extra activities section** includes suggestions for an in-class library, crossword and word search puzzles related to the novel, and extra vocabulary worksheets. There is a list of **bulletin board ideas** which gives the teacher suggestions for bulletin boards to go along with this unit. In addition, there is a list of **extra class activities** the teacher could choose from to enhance the unit or as a substitution for an exercise the teacher might feel is inappropriate for his/her class. Student materials may be reproduced for use in the teacher's classroom without infringement of copyrights. No other portions of this publication may be reproduced without the written consent of Teacher's Pet Publications, Inc.

UNIT OBJECTIVES - *The Red Badge of Courage*

1. Through reading Crane's *The Red Badge of Courage*, students will gain a better understanding of the "coming of age" theme as they are exposed to the path of the main character's personal growth to manhood.

2. Students will demonstrate their understanding of the text on four levels: factual, interpretive, critical and personal.

3. Students will recognize that conflicts within ourselves are a natural part of personal growth at any age in any historical era.

4. Students will study Crane's impressionistic style of writing.

5. Students will be exposed to the experiences of other war veterans who have been in combat.

6. Students will be given the opportunity to practice reading aloud and silently to improve their skills in each area.

7. Students will answer questions to demonstrate their knowledge and understanding of the main events and characters in *The Red Badge of Courage* as they relate to the author's theme development.

8. Students will enrich their vocabularies and improve their understanding of the novel through the vocabulary lessons prepared for use in conjunction with the novel.

9. The writing assignments in this unit are geared to several purposes:
    a. To have students demonstrate their abilities to inform, to persuade, or to express their own personal ideas
        Note: Students will demonstrate ability to write effectively to <u>inform</u> by developing and organizing facts to convey information. Students will demonstrate the ability to write effectively to <u>persuade</u> by selecting and organizing relevant information, establishing an argumentative purpose, and by designing an appropriate strategy for an identified audience. Students will demonstrate the ability to write effectively to <u>express personal ideas</u> by selecting a form and its appropriate elements.
    b. To check the students' reading comprehension
    c. To make students think about the ideas presented by the novel
    d. To encourage logical thinking
    e. To provide an opportunity to practice good grammar and improve students' use of the English language.

READING ASSIGNMENT SHEET - *The Red Badge of Courage*

Date Assigned	Assignment (Chapters)	Completion Date
	1-2	
	3-5	
	6-9	
	10-13	
	14-17	
	18-21	
	22-24	

UNIT OUTLINE - *The Red Badge of Courage*

1 Introduction P&V 1-2	2 Read 1-2 P&V 3-5	3 Study ?s 1-2 Read 3-5	4 Words! Worksheet	5 Study?s 3-5 PV&R 6-9 Assign PVR 10-17
6 Study ?s 6-9 Guest Speaker	7 Writing Assignment #1	8 Study ?s 10-17 PVR 18-24	9 Study ?s 18-24 Vocabulary	10 Extra Discussion Questions
11 Writing Conference Group Activity	12 Group Activity	13 Writing Assignment #2	14 Nonfiction Reading	15 Nonfiction Reports
16 Writing Assignment #3	17 Film	18 Film	19 Review	20 Test

Key: P = Preview Study Questions   V = Prereading Vocabulary Work   R = Read

STUDY GUIDE QUESTIONS

SHORT ANSWER STUDY GUIDE QUESTIONS - *The Red Badge of Courage*

Chapters 1-2
1. What news did the tall soldier bring from the river?
2. What was the reaction of each (the tall soldier, youthful private, and loud soldier) to the news?
3. What question caused the youthful soldier great concern?
4. From whose point of view is the story written?
5. What made Henry feel like a "mental outcast"?

Chapters 3 - 5
1. Why does Henry think "it would be better to get killed directly"?
2. What did the loud soldier give the young soldier at the end of Chapter 3? What do we learn about the loud soldier in that scene?
3. [The Officers] "neglected to stand in picturesque attitudes." What do we learn from this detail?
4. What was the outcome of the youth's first battle?

Chapters 6 - 9
1. What was the youth's opinion of himself after the first battle?
2. What "impossible thing" happened after the first battle?
3. Did the youth retreat at the second attack?
4. Why did the youth feel wronged?
5. Why did the squirrel's running make him feel better?
6. What did the youth find deep in the woods in the "chapel"?
7. Identify the tattered man.
8. Why didn't the youth want to talk to the tattered man?
9. The youth "wished that he, too, had a wound, a red badge of courage. "Why?
10. The youth meets Jim Conklin, the tall soldier, again in Chapter 9. What does Henry promise Jim?
11. What is the significance of
    a. the location of Jim's wounds?
    b. "The red sun was pasted in the sky like a <u>wafer</u>?"
    c. Jim's initials?

Chapters 10 - 13
1. Why did Henry leave the tattered man again?
2. Why did Henry wish he were dead?
3. What did the tattered man want from Henry? Why did he keep talking to Henry?
4. The main conflict of this chapter is Henry vs. Himself. Explain.
5. Henry is finally wounded. By whom and how?
6. How did Henry get back to his regiment?
7. Identify Wilson.

Red Badge Short Answer Study Questions Page 2

8. What was Henry's lie?
9. Why did Henry "fumble with the buttons on his jacket"?
10. Why is it significant that Henry asks Wilson where he's going to sleep and what he's going to sleep in?

Chapters 14 - 17

1. What change did Henry notice in Wilson?
2. What does Crane mean when he says, "Apparently the other [Wilson] had now climbed a peak of wisdom from which he could perceive himself a very wee thing"?
3. Why does Henry say "So?" at the end of the chapter?
4. Why and how was Henry's self-pride restored?
5. Henry thinks "he could leave much to chance." Explain.
6. Back in Chapter 10, Henry wished he were dead. Here at the end of Chapter 15, what is his attitude?
7. Why was Henry "dumbfounded" at hearing himself say, "Well, don't we fight like the devil . . . ."?
8. What made Henry "suddenly a modest person"?
9. "He had slept and, awakening, had found himself a knight." Explain.

Chapters 18 - 21

1. What information did Henry and Wilson bring back to the regiment after they had gone to look for water?
2. "The youth stared at the land in front of him. It's foliages now seemed to veil powers and horrors. "What does that mean?
3. Henry grabs the flag. "Because no harm could come to it, he endowed it with power. He kept near, as if it could be the saver of lives . . . ."Explain how Henry can think this as he grabs the flag from the dead color sergeant.
4. "The retreat of the mule drivers was a march of shame to him . . .He presently wrapped his heart in a cloak of pride and kept the flag erect." What does this tell us about Henry's character now?
5. After retreating, the regiment faces yet another chance battle, which it wins. What does this do for the morale?
6. This chapter ends with "And they were men." Explain.
7. What did the officer tell Col. MacChesnay?
8. How did the men react to the conversation between the officer and the Colonel?
9. What did Thompson tell Henry and Wilson and what effect did it have on them?

Red Badge Short Answer Study Questions Page 3

Chapters 22 - 24
1. In the battle in Chapter 22, Henry was "deeply absorbed as a spectator" with "serene self-confidence." Contrast this with his attitude in earlier battles.
2. What was Henry's goal in Chapter 23? Did he achieve it?
3. In this chapter, Henry evaluates himself. What does he decide about his public deeds in battle? His treatment of the tattered soldier?
4. "Yet gradually he mustered force to put the sin at a distance." What is the "sin"? Why is it important for him to put it at a distance?
5. "He was a man." Why? How is "man" defined in *The Red Badge of Courage*?

KEY: SHORT ANSWER STUDY GUIDE QUESTIONS - *The Red Badge of Courage*

Chapters 1-2

1. What news did the tall soldier bring from the river?
   The tall soldier brought news that the regiment would soon be moving.

2. What was the reaction of each (the tall soldier, youthful private, and loud soldier) to the news?
   The tall soldier was apparently glad to be bringing the news. The youthful private watched and listened to the other men and then went into his hut to think about what he had heard. The loud soldier argued with the tall soldier, saying the regiment would not move.

3. What question caused the youthful soldier great concern?
   The youthful soldier was worried that he might run from battle.

4. From whose point of view is the story written?
   The story is written from an omniscient point of view, but in most chapters we see things from Henry's perspective.

5. What made Henry feel like a "mental outcast"?
   No one else seemed to be worried about whether or not they would run from battle. Henry felt like the only one struggling with this personal problem.

Chapters 3 - 5

1. Why does Henry think "it would be better to get killed directly"?
   Henry thinks it would be better to be killed directly than to wonder and worry about what will happen.

2. What did the loud soldier give the young soldier at the end of Chapter 3? What do we learn about the loud soldier in that scene?
   The loud soldier gave the young soldier some personal things to take to his family since he thought he might be killed in the upcoming battle. We learn that the loud soldier recognizes he is not invincible, that he probably is very concerned about being in the war.

3. [The Officers] "neglected to stand in picturesque attitudes." What do we learn from this detail?
   Henry notices the officers are not standing the way they were in his romantic dreams. This detail foreshadows that war--real war--is going to be very different than Henry imagined.

4. What was the outcome of the youth's first battle?
   The youth did not run from battle, and his regiment appears to have had a victory.

Chapters 6 - 9

1. What was the youth's opinion of himself after the first battle?
   The youth was proud of himself after the first battle. He "went into an ecstasy of self-satisfaction."

2. What "impossible thing" happened after the first battle?
   The enemy attacked a second time.

3. Did the youth retreat at the second attack?
   Yes.

4. Why did the youth feel wronged?
   Henry felt wronged because he ran when he thought everyone else was running from battle. In fact, most of the regiment must have remained to fight, and they won the battle. He felt tricked into running and is therefore bitter about the victory since he was not a part of it.

5. Why did the squirrel's running make him feel better?
   The squirrel represents nature--the natural order of things. Henry tries to make himself feel better by rationalizing that running from battle was the natural response, the wise decision.

6. What did the youth find deep in the woods in the "chapel".
   The youth found a dead soldier in the "chapel."

7. Identify the tattered man.
   The tattered man was a wounded soldier in the regiment lost Henry walked with.

8. Why didn't the youth want to talk to the tattered man?
   Henry didn't want to talk to the tattered man because he didn't want to have to admit his cowardice and he didn't want to lie.

9. The youth "wished that he, too, had a wound, a red badge of courage." Why?
   Henry wished he had a wound because it would be an outward sign of his bravery. Not having a wound was a sign (to him) of his cowardice.

10. The youth meets Jim Conklin, the tall soldier, again in Chapter 9. What does Henry promise Jim?
    Henry promises not to let Jim die in the road.

11. What is the significance of
    a. the location of Jim's wounds?
    b. "The red sun was pasted in the sky like a <u>wafer</u>?"
    c. Jim's initials?

    Jim's wounds were at his hand and side. Some critics think that the location of the wounds along with Jim Conklin's initials (J.C.) and other religious overtones (including the quoted passage about the sun being like a wafer) all may combine to show Jim as a Christ figure in the novel.

<u>Chapters 10 - 13</u>

1. Why did Henry leave the tattered man again?
    Henry left the tattered man again because the tattered man kept asking him about his wound. Since Henry didn't have one and didn't want to discuss it, he left.

2. Why did Henry wish he were dead?
    If he were dead, Henry wouldn't have to face his embarrassing retreat, his lack of a wound, or the problems being in this war seems to create for him.

3. What did the tattered man want from Henry? Why did he keep talking to Henry?
    The tattered man wanted a friend. He just wanted someone to talk to--perhaps because he was lonely or wanted to take his mind off of his wounds.

4. The main conflict of this chapter is Henry vs. Himself. Explain.
    We spend almost the whole chapter reading Henry's thoughts as he goes through scene after scene of possible scenarios regarding his current dilemma. He has thought about his problem so much, he is really beginning to be his own worst enemy, so to speak. There is a tremendous conflict within Henry.

5. Henry is finally wounded. By whom and how?
    Henry held the arm of a man in retreat, in hopes of getting some information. The man hit Henry with his rifle to make him let go.

6. How did Henry get back to his regiment?
    A young, cheerful soldier came along and helped Henry find his regiment.

7. Identify Wilson.
    Wilson is the loud soldier from earlier chapters. In this chapter, he is the soldier (from Henry's old regiment) who befriends Henry.

8. What was Henry's lie?
    When he is asked about his wound, Henry says he was shot.

9. Why did Henry "fumble with the buttons on his jacket"?
   Henry fumbles with the buttons on his jacket because he is reminded of his lie and would prefer not to reply.

10. Why is it significant that Henry asks Wilson where he's going to sleep and what he's going to sleep in?
    Finally, Henry seems concerned about someone other than himself.

Chapters 14 - 17
1. What change did Henry notice in Wilson?
   Wilson had lost his youthful loudness and gained the self-confidence of a man.

2. What does Crane mean when he says, "Apparently the other [Wilson] had now climbed a peak of wisdom from which he could perceive himself a very wee thing"?
   Wilson had been through some experience which had shown him that he was not the best nor most important thing in the universe.

3. Why does Henry say "So?" at the end of the chapter?
   Henry takes what Wilson says personally and in a negative way (even though it doesn't seem to be meant that way). His defensive, "So?" shows his attitude.

4. Why and how was Henry's self-pride restored?
   Henry realizes that he still has the package Wilson gave him before the first battle. Having seen this self-confident soldier in a weakened and vulnerable state, Henry feels he has something to hold over Wilson. It makes Henry feel more confident.

5. Henry thinks "he could leave much to chance." Explain.
   A great deal of his last day had been developed by chance, and Henry thinks he came through those experiences with things being just fine in the end. He doesn't have to always be in control; "he had been taught that many obligations in life were easily avoided."

6. Back in Chapter 10, Henry wished he were dead. Here at the end of Chapter 15, what is his attitude?
   He is thinking of romantic war scenes with himself as the central, heroic figure.

7. Why was Henry "dumbfounded" at hearing himself say, "Well, don't we fight like the devil..."?
   Henry realizes for a moment that he ran instead of fighting, yet he is including himself with those who did "fight like the devil."

8. What made Henry "suddenly a modest person"?
   A sarcastic soldier, tired of hearing Henry complain, commented that maybe Henry fought the whole battle the day before. Henry realized what a fraud he was.

9. "He had slept and, awakening, had found himself a knight." Explain.
   During the next battle, Henry didn't think; he just reacted and fought. When he was done fighting, he realized he had become a hero.

Chapters 18 - 21

1. What information did Henry and Wilson bring back to the regiment after they had gone to look for water?
   They learned that they were being sent into a battle from which they were not expected to return alive.

2. "The youth stared at the land in front of him. It's foliages now seemed to veil powers and horrors." What does that mean?
   The battles taking place on the land beneath the trees were made of many individual parts. There were the obvious horror scenes of war, but also there were little things going on which gave individual men a strength to continue or a feeling of confidence or superiority.

3. Henry grabs the flag. "Because no harm could come to it, he endowed it with power. He kept near, as if it could be the saver of lives . . . ." Explain how Henry can think this as he grabs the flag from the dead color sergeant.
   Henry slips back to a bit of a romantic scene here. He gives the flag the power because the flag, the symbol of their cause, must go forward. Henry doesn't stop to think much about the dead color sergeant.

4. "The retreat of the mule drivers was a march of shame to him . . . He presently wrapped his heart in a cloak of pride and kept the flag erect." What does this tell us about Henry's character now?
   He is still ashamed and embarrassed by retreat, but he looks at a larger picture, a greater cause, and his regiment's successes to gather the pride he needs to hold that flag up straight.

5. After retreating, the regiment faces yet another chance battle, which it wins. What does this do for the morale?
   It helps their morale.

6. This chapter ends with "And they were men." Explain.
   They were no longer a green, youthful regiment. They had seen war--victory and defeat--and had grown older and wiser.

7. What did the officer tell Col. MacChesnay?
   The officer condemned the regiment for not advancing farther.

8. How did the men react to the conversation between the officer and the Colonel?
   They all know that they fought as well as they could, and they decide that the officer is a "lunkhead."

9. What did Thompson tell Henry and Wilson and what effect did it have on them?
   Thompson told Wilson and Henry that the Colonel said they should be major-generals for their performance in battle. They were both happy and grateful for the praise.

<u>Chapters 22 - 24</u>

1. In the battle in Chapter 22, Henry was "deeply absorbed as a spectator" with "serene self-confidence." Contrast this with his attitude in earlier battles.
   In earlier battles, Henry was so absorbed with his own problems, he hardly saw anything without it directly relating to himself and his problem. He had no self-confidence. These quoted words from Chapter 22 describe a far more adult soldier.

2. What was Henry's goal in Chapter 23? Did he achieve it?
   Henry wanted to get the enemy's flag. He does.

3. In this chapter, Henry evaluates himself. What does he decide about his public deeds in battle? His treatment of the tattered soldier?
   He decides his public deeds in battle were good and his treatment of the tattered soldier was bad.

4. "Yet gradually he mustered force to put the sin at a distance." What is the "sin"? Why is it important for him to put it at a distance?
   His "sin" is deserting the tattered soldier. He has to realize that no one is perfect, that everyone makes mistakes. He cannot let this sin consume him the way his retreat did at first. There is nothing he can do to fix his sin, so he just has to carry on and try to live a good life.

5. "He was a man." Why? How is "man" defined in *The Red Badge of Courage*?
   Henry had faced death and by facing it had learned how to lead a better life. "He felt a quiet manhood, nonassertive but of sturdy and strong blood. He knew that he would no more quail before his guides wherever they would point."

MULTIPLE CHOICE STUDY GUIDE/QUIZ QUESTIONS - *The Red Badge of Courage*

Chapters 1 - 2

1. What news did the tall soldier bring from the river?
    a. The enemy would be attacking soon.
    b. The regiment would soon be moving.
    c. There was no more drinking water.
    d. The regiment would have to stay there for several more weeks.

2. What was the reaction of the youthful private to the news?
    a. He went to his hut to think about it.
    b. He agreed with the loud soldier.
    c. He was overjoyed.
    d. He went to investigate the situation for himself

3. What question caused the youthful soldier great concern?
    a. He wondered if he would have enough ammunition.
    b. He wondered if he would run from battle.
    c. He wondered if the officers knew what they were doing.
    d. He wondered if his comrades would leave him alone in battle.

4. From whose point of view is the story written?
    a. Henry's
    b. Omniscient
    c. First Person
    d. A soldier who had been observing

5. What made Henry feel like a "mental outcast"?
    a. He was smarter than everyone else.
    b. He wasn't as smart as everyone else.
    c. He thought no one else was worried about running from battle.
    d. He was the only realist.

Red Badge Multiple Choice Study/Quiz Questions Page 2

Chapters 3 - 5

1. Why does Henry think "it would be better to get killed directly"?
    a. He would probably be killed eventually, so he might as well get it over with.
    b. He was worried he might have a grotesque, life-long injury
    c. He hated his life anyway.
    d. He'd rather be dead than wonder and worry about what will happen.

2. What did the loud soldier give the young soldier at the end of Chapter 3?
    a. A drink of whiskey
    b. Some good advice
    c. Personal things to take to his family
    d. A "good luck" charm

3. [The Officers] "neglected to stand in picturesque attitudes." What do we learn from this detail?
    a. Real war will be different from Henry's romantic dreams.
    b. The officers were negligent from the start.
    c. Henry didn't understand the officers' attitudes about war.
    d. The officers were ugly.

4. What was the outcome of the youth's first battle?
    a. He ran from battle, but his regiment won anyway.
    b. He ran from battle, and his regiment lost.
    c. He did not run from battle, and his regiment won.
    d. He did not run from battle, but his regiment lost.

Red Badge Multiple Choice Study/Quiz Questions Page 3

Chapters 6 - 9
1. What was the youth's opinion of himself after the first battle?
    a. He was disappointed.
    b. He was self-satisfied.
    c. He was angry.
    d. He was depressed.

2. What "impossible thing" happened after the first battle?
    a. Henry fainted from stress and relief.
    b. Henry's regiment got lost.
    c. The enemy attacked again.
    d. Henry discovered the loud soldier had been killed.

3. Why did the youth feel wronged?
    a. He ran when he thought everyone else was running, but, in fact, most of the regiment stayed and fought.
    b. Most men in the regiment deserted him and left him to fight without much help.
    c. No one believed him when he told them he had been separated from his unit.
    d. His commanding officer had promised him a transfer but never gave him one.

4. Why did the squirrel's running make him feel better?
    a. Henry was glad to see some creature unaffected by the war.
    b. It helped Henry rationalize his own flight from danger.
    c. He was glad to see that something could run, as he wished he could.
    d. The squirrel was something cute in an otherwise horrid environment.

5. What did the youth find deep in the woods in the "chapel."
    a. A grave
    b. An old cross
    c. A dead soldier
    d. Nothing that could be seen; just a peaceful feeling

6. Identify the tattered man.
    a. He was a dead soldier.
    b. He was a wounded soldier in the regiment with which lost Henry walked.
    c. He was Wilson.
    d. He was the loud soldier after the battle.

Red Badge Multiple Choice Study/Quiz Questions Page 4

7. Why didn't the youth want to talk to the tattered man?
    a. Henry didn't want to admit his cowardice.
    b. Henry was hurt too much to talk.
    c. The tattered man gave him the creeps.
    d. He didn't want to witness the tattered man's death.

8. The youth "wished that he, too, had a wound, a red badge of courage." Why?
    a. He felt like a mental outcast.
    b. He would then be able to go home.
    c. He wanted an outward sign of bravery.
    d. He wanted everyone to pity him.

9. The youth meets Jim Conklin, the tall soldier, again in Chapter 9. What does Henry promise Jim?
    a. To deliver papers to Jim's family
    b. To take care of Jim's family
    c. Not to let anyone take his clothes and boots
    d. Not to let Jim die in the road

10. What clue(s) to some critics use to show Jim as a Christ-figure?
    a. The location of his wounds
    b. His initials
    c. The religious overtones in passages related to Jim
    d. All of the above

Red Badge Multiple Choice Study/Quiz Questions Page 5

<u>Chapters 10 - 13</u>
1. Why did Henry leave the tattered man again?
   a. Henry didn't have a wound.
   b. Henry wanted to go talk to Jim.
   c. The tattered man was repulsive.
   d. All of the above

2. What did the tattered man want from Henry?
   a. Henry never found out what he wanted.
   b. A promise that he would not let him die in the road.
   c. Companionship
   d. His personal papers returned

3. What is the main conflict in the section?
   a. Man vs. Nature
   b. Man vs. Himself
   c. Man vs. Society
   d. Man vs. Man

4. How is Henry wounded?
   a. Henry is shot in the head.
   b. The bullet just grazes Henry's head.
   c. Henry runs into a tree and hurts his head.
   d. A soldier hits Henry in the head with his rifle.

5. How did Henry get back to his regiment?
   a. A young, cheerful soldier helped Henry.
   b. The tattered man told him where to go.
   c. An officer told him where to find his regiment.
   d. None of the above

6. Identify Wilson.
   a. He is the loud soldier.
   b. He is the tattered soldier.
   c. He is the officer.
   d. He is Henry.

Red Badge Multiple Choice Study/Quiz Questions Page 6

7. What was Henry's lie?
    a. Henry said he ran from the battle.
    b. Henry said Jim Conklin hit him.
    c. Henry said the tattered man shot him.
    d. Henry said he was shot.

8. Why did Henry "fumble with the buttons on his jacket"?
    a. His head hurts and he can't think straight.
    b. He is upset by recalling Jim's death.
    c. He is reminded of his life and would prefer not to reply.
    d. He doesn't know how to thank the men who have helped him.

9. Why is it significant that Henry asks Wilson where he's going to sleep and what he's going to sleep in?
    a. Henry doesn't trust Wilson.
    b. Finally, Henry seems concerned about someone other than himself.
    c. Henry was just making idle conversation.
    d. Henry wants to make sure Wilson doesn't use his (Henry's) sleeping bag.

Red Badge Multiple Choice Study/Quiz Questions Page 7

Chapters 14 - 17
1. What change did Henry notice in Wilson?
    a. Wilson looked considerably older and weaker.
    b. Wilson had grown a beard.
    c. Wilson had lost his youthful loudness and gained the self-confidence of a man.
    d. Wilson was more boastful than ever.

2. What does Crane mean when he says, "Apparently the other [Wilson] had now climbed a peak of wisdom from which he could perceive himself a very wee thing"?
    a. Wilson had fought in the mountains.
    b. Wilson had had some experience which had shown him he was not the best or most important thing in the universe.
    c. Wilson saw that he was not as tall as many of the other soldiers.
    d. There were two Wilsons in the unit, one of whom had learned his lesson.

3. Why and how was Henry's self-pride restored?
    a. He realizes he has something to "hold" over the self-confident Wilson.
    b. He proves his manhood in a fist fight with Wilson.
    c. He lies about his role in the battle to win the respect of the soldiers, and he truly believes he is actually a hero.
    d. He remembers the squirrel.

4. Henry thinks "he could leave much to chance." Why?
    a. Henry has never done much personal planning.
    b. Henry has to be in complete control of his destiny.
    c. A great deal of his last day was developed by chance, and things turned out okay for him.
    d. Everything is out of his control; he has given up his psychological warfare with himself in total defeat.

5. Back in Chapter 10, Henry wished he were dead. Here at the end of Chapter 15, what is his attitude?
    a. He still wishes he were dead.
    b. He is thinking of himself as a romantic war hero.
    c. He realizes he's just like everyone else--doing a dirty job in a dirty war.
    d. He wants to go home.

Red Badge Multiple Choice Study/Quiz Questions Page 8

6. Why was Henry "dumbfounded" at hearing himself say, "Well, don't we fight like the devil . . . ."?
    a. He is usually so introspective he doesn't say anything, he was amazed he was speaking much at all.
    b. He never spoke in such a common way before.
    c. He was filled with the spirit of the romantic glory of war.
    d. He realized that he ran instead of fighting but included himself with those who did fight.

7. What made Henry "suddenly a modest person"?
    a. He thought about Jim Conklin.
    b. He realized he was a fraud.
    c. Wilson showed him the wounds he got in battle.
    d. The officer reprimanded him.

8. "He had slept and, awakening, had found himself _____.
    a. Alone
    b. A fraud
    c. A knight
    d. Captured

Red Badge Multiple Choice Study/Quiz Questions Page 9

Chapters 18 - 21

1. What information did Henry and Wilson bring back to the regiment after they had gone to look for water?
    a. There was plenty of drinking water ahead.
    b. The enemy was about to attack.
    c. Their side was losing the war.
    d. They were being sent into a battle from which no one was expected to return.

2. "The youth stared at the land in front of him. Its foliages now seemed to veil _____."
    a. Powers and horrors
    b. The enemy
    c. The glory of war
    d. His regiment

3. Henry grabbed the flag. "Because no harm could come to it, he _____."
    a. Carried it to the rest of the troops
    b. Hid it to keep it safe
    c. Handed it to Wilson
    d. Endowed it with power

4. After retreating, the regiment faces yet another chance battle. What is the result of that battle?
    a. The regiment wins, and morale is boosted.
    b. The regiment loses, and morale sinks lower.
    c. The regiment is scattered and broken.
    d. The regiment is wiped out in the battle; only Henry and Wilson are left.

5. This chapter ends with "And they were men." Explain.
    a. There were no women in their regiment.
    b. They were no longer a green, youthful regiment; they had seen war and grown older and wiser.
    c. By the time of this battle, all the boys had had their 18th birthday.
    d. b and c

6. What did the officer tell Col. MacChesnay?
    a. He praised the unit for a job well done.
    b. He told the colonel that they were out of supplies and reinforcements.
    c. He told him to try to keep up morale among the soldiers.
    d. He condemned the regiment for not advancing further.

Red Badge Multiple Choice Study/Quiz Questions Page 10

7. How did the men react to the conversation between the officer and the Colonel?
    a. They plan to quit.
    b. They decide the officer is a lunkhead.
    c. They hope he gets killed in the next battle.
    d. They are embarrassed and decide to do better next time.

8. What did Thompson tell Henry and Wilson, and what effect did it have on them?
    a. They were the only ones who survived the battle.
    b. They could go home.
    c. The Colonel said they should be major generals.
    d. The Colonel said they were yellow bellied dogs.

Red Badge Multiple Choice Study/Quiz Questions Page 11

Chapters 22 - 24
1. How is Henry different during the battle in Chapter 22 as compared with his earlier battles?
    a. He is less introspective and more self-confident.
    b. He is more involved with his own problems than concerned with the battle.
    c. He doesn't care anymore.
    d. He has gone "battle-crazy."

2. What was Henry's goal in Chapter 23?
    a. Simply to stay alive
    b. To get to carry his regiment's flag
    c. To be better than Wilson
    d. To capture the enemy's flag

3. In this chapter, Henry evaluates himself. What does he decide?
    a. His public deeds in battle were good.
    b. His treatment of the tattered soldier was justifiable and okay.
    c. He still wishes he had been killed early on in the fighting.
    d. His life isn't worth living because of his shameful retreat and his unkind treatment of the tattered soldier.

4. "Yet gradually he mustered force to put the sin at a distance." What is the "sin"?
    a. Deserting his regiment
    b. Deserting the tattered soldier
    c. Not keeping his promise to Jim Conklin
    d. Not keeping his promise to Wilson

ANSWER KEY: MULTIPLE CHOICE STUDY/QUIZ QUESTIONS
The Red Badge of Courage

<u>Chapters 1-2</u>
1. B
2. A
3. B
4. B
5. C

<u>Chapters 3-5</u>
1. D
2. C
3. A
4. C

<u>Chapters 6-9</u>
1. B
2. C
3. A
4. B
5. C
6. B
7. A
8. C
9. D
10. D

<u>Chapters 10-13</u>
1. A
2. C
3. B
4. D
5. A
6. A
7. D
8. C
9. B

<u>Chapters 14-17</u>
1. C
2. B
3. A
4. C
5. B
6. D
7. B
8. C

<u>Chapters 18-21</u>
1. D
2. A
3. D
4. A
5. B
6. D
7. B
8. C

<u>Chapters 22-24</u>
1. A
2. D
3. A
4. B

PREREADING VOCABULARY WORKSHEETS

VOCABULARY - *The Red Badge of Courage*

Chapters 1-2 Part I: Using Prior Knowledge and Contextual Clues

Below are the sentences in which the vocabulary words above appear in the text. Read the sentence. Use any clues you can find in the sentence combined with your prior knowledge, and write what you think the underlined words mean on the lines provided.

1. For a time he was <u>obliged</u> to labor to make himself believe.

_____

2. Others spoke of tattered and eternally hungry men who fired <u>despondent</u> powders.

_____

3. Or, on the other hand, he might be a man heretofore doomed to peace and <u>obscurity</u>, but, in reality, made to shine in war.

_____

4. As he looked all about him and pondered upon the mystic gloom, he began to believe that at any moment the <u>ominous</u> distance might be aflare and the rolling crashes of an engagement come to his ears.

_____

5. He was despondent and <u>sullen</u>, and threw shifting glances about him.

_____

6. The youth, considering himself as separated from the others, was saddened by the <u>blithe</u> and merry speeches that went from rank to rank.

_____

7. The young girl, with pink cheeks and shining eyes, stood like a <u>dauntless</u> statue.

_____

8. "No, I ain't," exclaimed the loud solder <u>indignantly</u>; "and I didn't say I was the bravest man in the world, neither.

_____

Vocabulary - *The Red Badge of Courage* Chapters 1-2 page 2

Part II: Determining the Meaning

You have tried to figure out the meanings of the vocabulary words for Chapters 1-2. Now match the vocabulary words to their dictionary definitions. If there are words for which you cannot figure out the definition by contextual clues and by process of elimination, look them up in a dictionary.

___ 1. Obliged
___ 2. Despondent
___ 3. Obscurity
___ 4. Ominous
___ 5. Sullen
___ 6. Blithe
___ 7. Dauntless
___ 8. Indignantly

A. morose; sulky
B. caused to do something
C. fearless; bold
D. with an anger aroused by something unjust
E. the condition of being unknown
F. feeling disheartened or dejected
G. cheerful; casual; carefree
H. portentous; foreboding

Vocabulary - *The Red Badge of Courage* Chapters 3-5

Part I: Using Prior Knowledge and Contextual Clues
 Below are the sentences in which the vocabulary words above appear in the text. Read the sentence. Use any clues you can find in the sentence combined with your prior knowledge, and write what you think the underlined words mean on the lines provided.

1. There was a sudden change from the ponderous infantry of theory to the light and speedy infantry of practice.

_____

2. A house standing placidly in different fields had to him an ominous look

_____

3. The shadows of the woods were formidable.

_____

4. With the passionate song of the bullets and the banshee shrieks of shells were mingled loud catcalls and bits of facetious advice concerning places of safety.

_____

5. He suddenly lost concern for himself, and forgot to look at a menacing fate.

_____

6. If he had thought the regiment was about to be annihilated perhaps he could have amputated himself from it.

_____

7. He developed the acute exasperation of a pestered animal, a well-meaning cow worried by dogs.

_____

8. They lay twisted in fantastic contortions. Arms were bent and heads were turned in incredible ways.

_____

Vocabulary - *The Red Badge of Courage* Chapters 3-5 page 2

Part II: Determining the Meaning

You have tried to figure out the meanings of the vocabulary words for Chapters 3-5. Now match the vocabulary words to their dictionary definitions. If there are words for which you cannot figure out the definition by contextual clues and by process of elimination, look them up in a dictionary.

___ 9. Ponderous   A. arousing fear or dread; awesome; difficult to overtake
___ 10. Placidly   B. the state of extremely annoyed or irate
___ 11. Formidable   C. outwardly calm or composed; complacent
___ 12. Facetious   D. massive
___ 13. Menacing   E. humorous and flippant; playfully jocular
___ 14. Annihilated   F. characterized by being twisted or bent out of shape
___ 15. Exasperation   G. threatening
___ 16. Contortions   H. wiped out; destroyed completely

Vocabulary - *The Red Badge of Courage* Chapters 6-9

Part I: Using Prior Knowledge and Contextual Clues
 Below are the sentences in which the vocabulary words above appear in the text. Read the sentence. Use any clues you can find in the sentence combined with your prior knowledge, and write what you think the underlined words mean on the lines provided.

1. The red, formidable difficulties of war had been <u>vanquished</u>.

2. Into the youth's eyes there came a look that one can see in the <u>orbs</u> of a jaded horse.

3. The men there seemed to be in conventional moods, altogether unaware of the <u>impending</u> annihilation.

4. Perhaps the general, unable to comprehend <u>chaos</u>, might call upon him for information.

5. It suddenly occurred to the youth that the fight in which he had been was, after all, but <u>perfunctory</u> popping.

6. The sergeant, taking not of this, gave pause to his elaborate history while he administered a <u>sardonic</u> comment. "Be keerful, honey, you'll be a-ketchin' flies," he said.

7. He became again the grim, stalking <u>specter</u> of a soldier.

8. Then it was shaken by a prolonged <u>ague</u>. He stared into space.

Vocabulary - *The Red Badge of Courage* Chapters 6-9 page 2

Part II: Determining the Meaning

You have tried to figure out the meanings of the vocabulary words for Chapters 6-9. Now match the vocabulary words to their dictionary definitions. If there are words for which you cannot figure out the definition by contextual clues and by process of elimination, look them up in a dictionary.

___ 17. Vanquished   A. mocking
___ 18. Orbs   B. a recurrent chill or fit of shivering
___ 19. Impending   C. defeated; overcome
___ 20. Chaos   D. likely to happen soon
___ 21. Perfunctory   E. ghost
___ 22. Sardonic   F. total disorder or confusion
___ 23. Specter   G. acting with little interest or care
___ 24. Ague   H. eyes

Vocabulary - *The Red Badge of Courage* Chapters 10-13

Part I: Using Prior Knowledge and Contextual Clues
　　Below are the sentences in which the vocabulary words above appear in the text. Read the sentence. Use any clues you can find in the sentence combined with your prior knowledge, and write what you think the underlined words mean on the lines provided.

1. From the heaving tangle issued exhortations, commands, imprecations.

_____

2. Avoiding the obstructions gave it the sinuous movement of a serpent.

_____

3. He searched about in his mind for an adequate malediction for the indefinite cause, the thing
　 upon which men turn the words of final blame.

_____

4. In a defeat there would be a roundabout vindication of himself. He thought it would prove,
　 in a manner, that he had fled early because of his superior powers of perception.

_____

5. They were heedless of his appeals. They did not seem to see him.

_____

6. There was a mighty altercation.

_____

7. . . . then he heard a cheerful and audacious whistling as the man strode away.

_____

8. After the reproof the youth said no more.

_____

Vocabulary - *The Red Badge of Courage* Chapters 10-13 page 2

Part II: Determining the Meaning

You have tried to figure out the meanings of the vocabulary words for Chapters 10-13. Now match the vocabulary words to their dictionary definitions. If there are words for which you cannot figure out the definition by contextual clues and by process of elimination, look them up in a dictionary.

___ 25. Imprecations   A. heated or noisy quarrel
___ 26. Sinuous   B. the evidence or argument that justifies an act
___ 27. Malediction   C. arrogantly insolent
___ 28. Vindication   D. winding
___ 29. Heedless   E. reprimand
___ 30. Altercation   F. curses
___ 31. Audacious   G. to curse or slander
___ 32. Reproof   H. paying little or no attention; unmindful

Vocabulary - *The Red Badge of Courage* Chapters 14-17

Part I: Using Prior Knowledge and Contextual Clues

Below are the sentences in which the vocabulary words above appear in the text. Read the sentence. Use any clues you can find in the sentence combined with your prior knowledge, and write what you think the underlined words mean on the lines provided.

1. There was about him now a fine reliance.

_____

2. The youth was quite disconcerted at this surprising reception of his remarks.

_____

3. The latter felt immensely superior to his friend, but he inclined to condescension.

_____

4. He presently began a long and intricate denunciation of the commander of the forces.

_____

5. Inwardly he was reduced to an abject pulp by these chance words.

_____

6. In the regiment there was a peculiar kind of hesitation denoted in the attitudes of the men.

_____

7. For today he felt that he had earned opportunities for contemplative repose.

_____

Vocabulary - *The Red Badge of Courage* Chapters 14-17 page 2

Part II: Determining the Meaning

You have tried to figure out the meanings of the vocabulary words for Chapters 14-17. Now match the vocabulary words to their dictionary definitions. If there are words for which you cannot figure out the definition by contextual clues and by process of elimination, look them up in a dictionary.

___ 33. Reliance   A. the act of coming down voluntarily to the level of inferiors
___ 34. Disconcerted   B. confidence; dependence; trust
___ 35. Condescension   C. lacking self composure
___ 36. Denunciation   D. wretched; of the most contemptible kind
___ 37. Abject   E. an open condemnation or censure
___ 38. Denoted   F. rest
___ 39. Repose   G. marked; indicated; signified

Vocabulary - *The Red Badge of Courage* Chapters 18-21

Part I: Using Prior Knowledge and Contextual Clues
   Below are the sentences in which the vocabulary words above appear in the text. Read the sentence. Use any clues you can find in the sentence combined with your prior knowledge, and write what you think the underlined words mean.

1. The voices of the cannon were mingled in a long and interminable row.

_____

2. There was the delirium that encounters despair and death, and is heedless and blind to the odds.

_____

3. . . . and off to the right an ominous demonstration could sometimes be dimly discerned.

_____

4. . . . and then with a long, wailful cry the dilapidated regiment surged forward and began its new journey.

_____

5. The dead man, swinging with bended back, seemed to be obstinately tugging, in ludicrous and awful ways, for the possession of the flag.

_____

6. . . . it was derived that they had been unaware of the proximity of their dark-suited foes or had mistaken the direction.

_____

7. The impetus of enthusiasm was theirs again.

_____

8. The youth in this contemplation was smitten with a large astonishment.

_____

Vocabulary - *The Red Badge of Courage* Chapters 18-21 page 2

Part II: Determining the Meaning

    You have tried to figure out the meanings of the vocabulary words for Chapters 18-21. Now match the vocabulary words to their dictionary definitions. If there are words for which you cannot figure out the definition by contextual clues and by process of elimination, look them up in a dictionary.

___ 40. Interminably   A. closeness
___ 41. Delirium   B. afflicted
___ 42. Discerned   C. impelling force; impulse; stimulus
___ 43. Dilapidated   D. laughable because of obvious absurdity or incongruity
___ 44. Ludicrous   E. broken down, falling apart; ruined
___ 45. Proximity   F. endless
___ 46. Impetus   G. detected; perceived
___ 47. Smitten   H. temporary mental confusion; a state of uncontrolled emotion or excitement

Vocabulary - *The Red Badge of Courage* Chapters 22-24

Part I: Using Prior Knowledge and Contextual Clues
  Below are the sentences in which the vocabulary words above appear in the text. Read the sentence. Use any clues you can find in the sentence combined with your prior knowledge, and write what you think the underlined words mean on the lines provided.

1. Having stirred this prodigious uproar, ... the brigade, after a little time, came marching airily out again.

_____

2. ... he saw wild and desperate rushes of men perpetually backward and forward in riotous surges.

_____

3. But at one part of the line there was a grim and obdurate group that made no movement.

_____

4. The third captive sat with a morose countenance.

_____

5. For a time this pursuing recollection of the tattered man took all elation from the youth's veins.

_____

6. The procession of weary soldiers became a bedraggled train, despondent and muttering, marching with churning effort in a trough of liquid brown mud under a low, wretched sky.

_____

Vocabulary - *The Red Badge of Courage* Chapters 22-24 page 2

Part II: Determining the Meaning

You have tried to figure out the meanings of the vocabulary words for Chapters 22-24. Now match the vocabulary words to their dictionary definitions. If there are words for which you cannot figure out the definition by contextual clues and by process of elimination, look them up in a dictionary.

___ 48. Prodigious
___ 49. Perpetually
___ 50. Obdurate
___ 51. Morose
___ 52. Incorrigible
___ 53. Elation
___ 54. Bedraggled

A. continually
B. enormous; extraordinary; marvelous
C. intractable; not giving in
D. Made wet and limp
E. melancholy
F. unmanageable
G. Exalted feeling arising from a sense of triumph power or relief

ANSWER KEY - VOCABULARY
The Red Badge of Courage

Chapters 1-2	Chapters 3-5	Chapters 6-9	Chapters 10-13	Chapters 14-17
1. B	9. D	17. C	25. F	33. B
2. F	10. C	18. H	26. D	34. C
3. E	11. A	19. D	27. G	35. A
4. H	12. E	20. F	28. B	36. E
5. A	13. G	21. G	29. H	37. D
6. G	14. H	22. A	30. A	38. G
7. C	15. B	23. E	31. C	39. F
8. D	16. F	24. B	32. E	

Chapters 18-21	Chapters 22-24
40. F	48. B
41. H	49. A
42. G	50. C
43. E	51. E
44. D	52. F
45. A	53. G
46. C	54. D
47. B	

DAILY LESSONS

LESSON ONE

Objectives
1. To introduce *The Red Badge of Courage* unit.
2. To distribute books and other related materials
3. To preview the study questions for chapters 1-2
4. To familiarize students with the vocabulary for chapters 1-2

Activity #1

If you are able to find one, show a few minutes of a "bloopers" tape, a tape of out-takes or mistakes--even some kind of a sports bloopers tape will do to illustrate the point. After showing the tape (a few minutes--not the whole class period), ask students to share some of their favorite bloopers that they have seen or have done themselves.

TRANSITION: Bloopers are often funny to see. Sometimes they are funny to both the person doing the blooper as well as the audience. Sometimes bloopers aren't very funny at all; they're embarrassing. And sometimes we do things that are more serious than bloopers--things we worry about and wish we could take back. Have you ever said something or done something to someone and wished you hadn't? (Leave time for student discussion.)

Sometimes people make huge mistakes which ruin their careers or even alter the course of their whole lives. Can you think of some examples of these kinds of things? (Leave time for student discussion.)

Sometimes we even get a little paranoid and start worrying about things we might do wrong and be embarrassed about--things we haven't even done yet. For example, if you play on a sports team, you might worry about dropping the ball or tripping on the field. Then you get so nervous thinking about the possibility of making an embarrassing mistake that you actually do it. Has that kind of thing ever happened to you? (Leave time for class discussion.)

These are some of the kinds of things that happen to Henry when he goes off to war in the book we are going to read, *The Red Badge of Courage*. Henry goes off to war, the American Civil War, and worries about how he will perform in a battlefield situation, actually under fire. It is the story of his self-doubt, his thoughts, and actions in his first few battles.

Activity #2

Distribute the materials students will use in this unit. Explain in detail how students are to use these materials.

Study Guides Students should read the study guide questions for each reading assignment prior to beginning the reading assignment to get a feeling for what events and ideas are important in the section they are about to read. After reading the section, students will (as a class or individually) answer the questions to review the important events and ideas from that section of the book. Students should keep the study guides as study materials for the unit test.

Vocabulary   Prior to reading a reading assignment, students will do vocabulary work related to the section of the book they are about to read. Following the completion of the reading of the book, there will be a vocabulary review of all the words used in the vocabulary assignments. Students should keep their vocabulary work as study materials for the unit test.

Reading Assignment Sheet   You need to fill in the reading assignment sheet to let students know by when their reading has to be completed. You can either write the assignment sheet up on a side blackboard or bulletin board and leave it there for students to see each day, or you can "ditto" copies for each student to have. In either case, you should advise students to become very familiar with the reading assignments so they know what is expected of them.

Extra Activities Center   The Extra Activities page of this unit contains suggestions for an extra library of related books and articles in your classroom as well as crossword and word search puzzles. Make an extra activities center in your room where you will keep these materials for students to use. (Bring the books and articles in from the library and keep several copies of the puzzles on hand.) Explain to students that these materials are available for students to use when they finish reading assignments or other class work early.

Nonfiction Assignment Sheet   Explain to students that they each are to read at least one non-fiction piece from the library during this unit. Students will fill out a nonfiction assignment sheet after completing the reading to help you evaluate their reading experiences and to help the students think about and evaluate their own reading experiences.

Books   Each school has its own rules and regulations regarding student use of school books. Advise students of the procedures that are normal for your school.

Activity #3

Preview the study questions and have students do the vocabulary work for Chapters 1-2 of *The Red Badge of Courage*. If students do not finish this assignment during this class period, they should complete it prior to the next class meeting.

NONFICTION ASSIGNMENT SHEET
(To be completed after reading the required nonfiction article)

Name _____ Date _____

Title of Nonfiction Read _____

Written By _____ Publication Date _____

I. Factual Summary: Write a short summary of the piece you read.

II. Vocabulary
    1. With which vocabulary words in the piece did you encounter some degree of difficulty?

    2. How did you resolve your lack of understanding with these words?

III. Interpretation: What was the main point the author wanted you to get from reading his work?

IV. Criticism
    1. With which points of the piece did you agree or find easy to accept? Why?

    2. With which points of the piece did you disagree or find difficult to believe? Why?

V. Personal Response: What do you think about this piece? <u>OR</u> How does this piece influence your ideas?

LESSON TWO

Objectives
1. To read chapters 1-2
2. To give students practice reading orally
3. To evaluate students' oral reading

Activity #1

Have students read chapters 1-2 of *The Red Badge of Courage* out loud in class. You probably know the best way to get readers with your class; pick students at random, ask for volunteers, or use whatever method works best for your group. If you have not yet completed an oral reading evaluation for your students this marking period, this would be a good opportunity to do so. A form is included with this unit for your convenience.

If students do not complete reading chapters 1-2 in class, they should do so prior to your next class meeting.

Activity #2

Also prior to the next class meeting students should preview the study questions and do the vocabulary work for chapters 3-5.

LESSON THREE

Objectives
1. To review the main ideas and events of chapters 1-2
2. To read chapters 3-5
3. To complete the oral reading evaluations

Activity #1

Give students a few minutes to formulate answers for the study guide questions for chapters 1-2 and then discuss the answers to the questions in detail. Write the answers on the board or overhead transparency so students can have the correct answers for study purposes. NOTE: It is a good practice in public speaking and leadership skills for individual students to take charge of leading the discussions of the study questions. Perhaps a different student could go to the front of the class and lead the discussion each day that the study questions are discussed during this unit. Of course, the teacher should guide the discussion when appropriate and be sure to fill in any gaps the students leave.

Activity #2

Have students read chapters 3-5 orally in class. If you have not yet completed the oral reading evaluations, do so during this class period.

ORAL READING EVALUATION - *Red Badge of Courage*

Name _____ Class____ Date _____

SKILL	EXCELLENT	GOOD	AVERAGE	FAIR	POOR
Fluency	5	4	3	2	1
Clarity	5	4	3	2	1
Audibility	5	4	3	2	1
Pronunciation	5	4	3	2	1
_____	5	4	3	2	1
_____	5	4	3	2	1

Total _____ Grade _____

Comments:

LESSON FOUR

Objectives
    1. To show students how Crane uses descriptive words, active verbs, comparisons, personifications, details, and descriptive nouns to make his story come to life
    2. To get students to think about the connotations of the words Crane chooses and the effects of the words on the images he creates

Activity #1
    Distribute the Words! Words! Words! worksheet. Students should take a few minutes to look over the passages in part one, underlining the descriptive words and phrases. After students have had time to consider the passages, examine and discuss the images Crane creates. Explore his word choices and the writing devices he uses to create graphic images. Look at the connotations of the words he uses, and ask students why he used those specific words. Ask students for synonyms to those descriptive words and see if any synonyms would have been better choices.

Activity #2
After thoroughly discussing the use of words, descriptive phrases and figurative language in these passages, give students time to complete part 2 of the worksheet–writing a descriptive paragraph of their own.

Optional Activity
    Continue pointing out descriptive language throughout the rest of the novel. Perhaps each student could be responsible for pointing out exceptionally descriptive passages in each chapter or in a certain group of pages. Then, as you do the study questions and answers, you could add in a discussion of the descriptive language.
    Assign one chapter of the book (24 chapters total) to each of your students. Tell students that they should jot down all references to any colors in their chapters. Allow students ample time to complete this task, then make a chart on the board (or overhead) with one column for each color. Under each color in each column write down the examples students give.
    After the chart is completed, go back and do an analysis of the chart with your students. How does Stephen Crane use colors in the book to create images and moods? Do some colors even take on a symbolic significance? Lead a thorough discussion of the use of color in *The Red Badge of Courage*.

WORDS, WORDS, WORDS! WORKSHEET
The Red Badge of Courage

Part 1

In The Red Badge of Courage, Stephen Crane includes many highly descriptive passages. Below are several examples from the first five chapters of the book. Underline the most descriptive words and phrases to prepare for a discussion of these passages.

Some talked of gray, bewiskered hordes who were advancing with relentless curses and chewing tobacco with unspeakable valor; tremendous bodies of fierce soldiery who were sweeping along like the Huns. Others spoke of tattered and eternally hungry men who fired despondent powders. (Chapter 1)

A little panic-fear grew in his mind. As his imagination went forward to a fight, he saw hideous possibilities. He contemplated the lurking menaces of the future, and failed in an effort to see himself standing stoutly in the midst of them. He recalled his visions of broken-bladed glory, but in the shadow of the impending tumult, he suspected them to be impossible pictures. (Chapter 1)

He lay down in the grass. The blades pressed tenderly against his cheek. The moon had been lighted and was hung in a treetop. The liquid stillness of the night enveloping him made him feel vast pity for himself. There was a caress in the soft winds; and the whole mood of the darkness, he thought, was one of sympathy for himself in his distress. (Chapter 2)

A house standing placidly in distant fields had to him an ominous look. The shadows of the woods were formidable. He was certain that in this vista there lurked fierce-eyed hosts. . . . Suddenly those close forests would bristle with rifle barrels. Ironlike brigades would appear in the rear. . . . The enemy would presently swallow the whole command. He glared about him, expecting to see the stealthy approach of his death. (Chapter 3)

The din in front swelled to a tremendous chorus. The youth and his fellows were frozen to silence. They could see a flag that tossed in the smoke angrily. Near it were the blurred and agitated forms of troops. There came a turbulent stream of men across the fields. . . . A shell screaming like a storm banshee went over the huddled heads of the reserves. It landed in the grove, and exploding redly flung the brown earth. There was a little shower of pine needles. . . . Bullets began to whistle among the branches and nip a the trees. Twigs and leaves came sailing down. It was as if a thousand axes, wee and invisible, were being wielded. (Chapter IV)

Words, Words, Words! Worksheet Continued
The Red Badge of Courage

The battle reflection that shone for an instant in the faces on the mad current made the youth feel that forceful hands from heaven would not have been able to have held him in place if he could have got intelligent control of his legs. . . . There was an appalling imprint upon these faces. The struggle in the smoke had pictured an exaggeration of itself on the bleached cheeks and in the eyes wild with one desire. . . .The sight of this stampede exerted a floodlike force that seemed able to drag sticks and stones and men from the ground. (Chapter IV)

The guns squatted in a row like savage chiefs. They argued with abrupt violence. It was a grim pow-wow. Their busy servants ran hither and thither. (Chapter V)

Batteries were speaking with thunderous oratorical effect. Here and there there were flags, the red in the stripes dominating. They splashed bits of warm color upon the dark lines of the troops. . . . The youth felt the old thrill at the sight of the emblems. They were like beautiful birds strangely undaunted in a storm. (Chapter V)

Part 2
Write a descriptive paragraph about a sporting event in which you have participated or one you have observed. Try to use graphic, visual imagery the way Crane did in the passages above.

LESSON FIVE

Objectives
1. To review the main ideas and events from chapters 3-5
2. To preview the study questions for chapters 6-9
3. To preview the vocabulary words for chapters 6-9
4. To read chapters 6-9
5. To assign the previewing and reading work for chapters 10-17

Activity #1
Give students a few minutes to formulate answers for the study guide questions for chapters 3-5, and then discuss the answers to the questions in detail. Write the answers on the board or overhead transparency so students can have the correct answers for study purposes.

Activity #2
Tell students that during this class period they are to do the previewing work for chapters 6-9 and then read those chapters silently. In addition, when they finish this assignment, they are to do the previewing work for chapters 10-13 and 14-17. This work and the reading of these chapters should be done prior to Lesson Eight. (Give students a day and a date.)

LESSON SIX

Objectives
1. To review the main ideas and events of chapters 6-9
2. To broaden students' understanding of what it means to be in a war
3. To give students some fuel to start their next writing assignment

Activity #1
Take time to discuss the answers to the study questions for chapters 6-9.

Activity #2
Look in your local area for people who have actually been in a combat situation. Your local chapter of the VFW would be a good place to start your search. If you live close to a military installation, that would be another good source. Ask for a few volunteers to talk with your class about what it is really like to be in war. During this class period have your guests tell your class about some of their wartime experiences and give your students the opportunity to ask questions (if your guests agree to answer questions from students).

If no volunteers are available, consider showing a portion of The Civil War which aired on PBS. It has some excellent personal accounts of individuals' experiences in the war.

LESSON SEVEN

Objectives
1. To give students the opportunity to write their own personal opinions
2. To have students put themselves in Henry's shoes; to think about how they would react if they went to war
3. To give the teacher the opportunity to evaluate students' writing skills
4. To bring the story closer home to students

Activity #1
Distribute Writing Assignment #1. Discuss the directions in detail and give students an appropriate amount of time to complete the assignment. Collect the papers for grading.

Activity #2
If students finish the assignment early, they should complete the assignment from Lesson Five (preview and reading work for chapters 10-17). Remind students that the work for chapters 10-17 must be completed prior to your next class meeting.

LESSON EIGHT

Objectives
1. To review the main ideas and events in chapters 10-17
2. To preview the study questions for chapters 18-21 & 22-24
3. To preview the vocabulary for chapters 18-21 & 22-24
4. To read chapters 18-24

Activity #1
Discuss the study questions for chapters 10-17. You may wish to approach the questions as a quiz to make sure all students did the reading assignment.

Activity #2
Explain to students that they are to complete the preview and reading work for chapters 18-24 prior to your next class meeting. Give students the remainder of this class period to begin working on this assignment.

Activity #3
Explain to students that you will have writing conferences in the next class period. During the writing conference, you will discuss students' writing skills with them individually, based on their first writing assignments in this unit.

WRITING ASSIGNMENT #1 - *The Red Badge of Courage*

PROMPT

This writing assignment is to give you practice writing your own opinions and ideas. In *The Red Badge of Courage* and from other first-hand accounts, you have read and heard some people's opinions about what it is like to be in combat.

Considering all you have heard and your knowledge of yourself, write a composition in which you explain how you think you would react in a combat situation.

PREWRITING

One way to start is to think about the accounts you have heard. Jot down the main points that impressed you about being in combat. Now stop and think about yourself for a minute. Next to each of the points you wrote on the paper, jot down a few notes about how you think you would react to each of those aspects of combat.

DRAFTING

Look at what you have written down. Based on these notes, do you think you would be able to handle a combat situation well, just okay, or not at all? This statement then becomes your main idea. Write an introductory paragraph in which you include this main idea.

Each of the paragraphs in the body of your paper could deal with the main points you jotted down when prewriting. You could make one paragraph for your first point, in which you describe that aspect of war, what you believe your reaction to it would be, and reasons why you believe you would react that way. Do the same for each of the other points.

Then write a concluding paragraph in which you summarize your ideas and give your final thoughts on what you think your reaction in combat would be.

PROMPT

When you finish the rough draft of your paper, ask a student who sits near you to read it. After reading your rough draft, he/she should tell you what he/she liked best about your work, which parts were difficult to understand, and ways in which your work could be improved. Reread your paper considering your critic's comments and make the corrections you think are necessary.

PROOFREADING

Do a final proofreading of your paper double-checking your grammar, spelling, organization, and the clarity of your ideas.

LESSON NINE

Objectives
1. To review the main ideas and events of chapters 18-24
2. To review all the prereading vocabulary work

Activity #1
Discuss the answers to the study guide questions for chapters 18-24. Write the answers on the board for students to copy down for study use later.

Activity #2
Choose one (or more) of the vocabulary review activities listed on the next page and spend your class period as directed in the activity. Some of the materials for these review activities are located in the Vocabulary Resources section of this unit.

NOTE: If your students need more time to work with these vocabulary words, add an extra vocabulary day or use some of the extra materials as homework assignments to help them study.

VOCABULARY REVIEW ACTIVITIES

1. Divide your class into two teams and have an old-fashioned spelling or definition bee.

2. Give each of your students (or students in groups of two, three or four) a *The Red Badge of Courage* Vocabulary Word Search Puzzle. The person (group) to find all of the vocabulary words in the puzzle first wins.

3. Give students a *The Red Badge of Courage* Vocabulary Word Search Puzzle without the word list. The person or group to find the most vocabulary words in the puzzle wins.

4. Use a *The Red Badge of Courage* Vocabulary Crossword Puzzle. Put the puzzle onto a transparency on the overhead projector (so everyone can see it), and do the puzzle together as a class.

5. Give students a *The Red Badge of Courage* Vocabulary Matching Worksheet to do.

6. Divide your class into two teams. Use *The Red Badge of Courage* vocabulary words with their letters jumbled as a word list. Student 1 from Team A faces off against Student 1 from Team B. You write the first jumbled word on the board. The first student (1A or 1B) to unscramble the word wins the chance for his/her team to score points. If 1A wins the jumble, go to student 2A and give him/her a definition. He/she must give you the correct spelling of the vocabulary word which fits that definition. If he/she does, Team A scores a point, and you give student 3A a definition for which you expect a correctly spelled matching vocabulary word. Continue giving Team A definitions until some team member makes an incorrect response. An incorrect response sends the game back to the jumbled-word face off, this time with students 2A and 2B. Instead of repeating giving definitions to the first few students of each team, continue with the student after the one who gave the last incorrect response on the team. For example, if Team B wins the jumbled-word face-off, and student 5B gave the last incorrect answer for Team B, you would start this round of definition questions with student 6B, and so on. The team with the most points wins!

7. Have students write a story in which they correctly use as many vocabulary words as possible. Have students read their compositions orally! Post the most original compositions on your bulletin board.

LESSON TEN

Objective
  To discuss *The Red Badge of Courage* on interpretive and critical levels.

Activity #1
  Choose the questions from the Extra Discussion Questions/Writing Assignments which seem most appropriate for your students. A class discussion of these questions is most effective if students have been given the opportunity to formulate answers to the questions prior to the discussion. To this end, you may either have all the students formulate answers to all the questions, divide your class into groups and assign one or more questions to each group, or you could assign one question to each student in your class. The option you choose will make a difference in the amount of class time needed for this activity.

Activity #2
  After students have had ample time to formulate answers to the questions, begin your class discussion of the questions and the ideas presented by the questions. Be sure students take notes during the discussion so they have information to study for the unit test.

A FEW NOTES ABOUT *The Red Badge of Courage*

I. Biography of Crane
- Born 1871 Newark, NJ.
- 14th (and last) child in family.
- Father was Rev. Jonathan Crane, Methodist minister.
- Was noted for skepticism, kindness, and devotion to animals and sports.
- At college he focused on baseball, pool and poker.
- 1893 published *Maggie: A Girl of the Streets* pseudonymously.
- 1895 published *The Red Badge of Courage* as a book.
- 1897-98 wrote "The Open Boat," " The Bride Comes to Yellow Sky" and "The Blue Hotel."
- Met Cora Howorth Stewart (or Cora Taylor) and enjoyed her company and conversation. They stayed together.
- Traveled as a reporter to Mexico, Greece, Cuba, Puerto Rico, among other places.
- March 1900 leaned over to pat a dog and found his mouth full of blood. Died 3 months later.

II. Conflicts in *The Red Badge of Courage*
- Man vs. Himself - Henry's internal struggle
- Man vs. Nature - The soldiers out in the elements, in the forest; their physical needs for food, water, etc.
- Man vs. Man - the battle itself and the soldiers' struggle among themselves arguing
- Romantic vs. Realistic - Henry's romantic ideas of war and heroes versus the reality of a not-so-pretty nor so heroic war

III. Point of View
- Story is written from the omniscient point of view although we mostly see things from Henry's perspective.
- There are lots of references to point of view in the novel, as if point of view were itself a theme
- perhaps that a person's point of view determines their own reality.
- Some point of view references:
  a. Chapter 8, ¶ 7 "Reflecting, he saw a sort of humor in the point of view of himself and his fellow during the late encounter."
  b. Chapter 14, ¶ 15 "Apparently, the other had now climbed a peak of wisdom from which he could perceive himself as a very wee thing."
  c. Chapter 22, ¶ 13 "He was deeply absorbed as a spectator."
  d. Chapter 24, ¶ 14 "From this present view point he was enabled to look upon them in spectator fashion and to criticize them with some correctness, for his new condition had already defeated certain sympathies."
  e. Chapter 24, ¶ 15 "He spent delightful minutes viewing the gilded images of memory."

IV. Structure of the novel
    Chapters 1 - 5 Henry as thoughtful youth vs. rowdy and common regiment
    Chapters 6 - 12 Henry is introduced to death in war and nature
    Chapters 13 - 16 Wilson has matured; Henry is still an adolescent
    Chapters 17 - 23 Henry matures and joins the battle on Wilson's level; they both join completely with the regiment.
    Chapter 24 Henry reflects on his experiences and summarizes his thoughts.

EXTRA WRITING ASSIGNMENTS AND/OR DISCUSSION QUESTIONS
The Red Badge of Courage

Interpretive
1. Summarize the actual events of the plot. What does Henry do for the couple of days we follow him in the war?
2. Where is the climax of the story? Explain your choice.
3. Are the characters in *Red Badge* stereotypes? If so, explain the usefulness of employing stereotypes in the story. If they are not, explain how they merit individuality.
4. What are the conflicts in the story, and how are they resolved?
5. Discuss the importance of the setting of the story.
6. Why does Henry lie? How does he feel about doing it?

Critical
7. Explain the significance of the title of *The Red Badge of Courage*.
8. Describe Crane's writing style and its effects on the reader and the story.
9. Explain why the characters have two names, one general and one specific. (For example, Henry is the youth.)
10. How does Henry change during the course of the story?
11. Why is Jim Conklin included in the story? What does his character add?
12. Compare and contrast Henry Fleming and Wilson.
13. What is the importance of the Tattered Man?
14. Discuss the use of realism and romanticism in the story.
15. What is the main theme of *The Red Badge of Courage*?
16. Discuss Crane's use of religious imagery and symbolism in *Red Badge*. What does it add to the story?
17. What is Naturalism, and how does Stephen Crane use it in this story?

Personal Response
18. If *The Red Badge of Courage* had been written in the first person (if Henry were a narrator and our only source of information), how would that have changed the story and its effect?
19. Is the story of *The Red Badge of Courage* believable? Explain why or why not.
20. *The Red Badge of Courage* is a short novel. Could anything have been gained by including more scenes from the time before or after the events of the story? If so, what could have been added and for what purpose? If not, explain why not.
21. Define the word "courage."
22. Is Henry a hero?
23. Was it so wrong for Henry to leave the Tattered Man?

LESSON ELEVEN

Objectives
1. To personally give students feedback about their writing skills
2. To review the main events of the story and Henry's character development
3. To get students to synthesize the elements of the story

Activity
Divide your class into groups of four students. Explain to students that the class is going to have a hearing--a mini-trial. It is one week after the conclusion of the story of *The Red Badge of Courage* and the authorities have found out that Henry Fleming went AWOL during his second battle.

Divide your groups equally between prosecution and defense. Groups who represent the defense are to review the events of the story to defend Henry's actions and to keep him from being convicted of desertion. Groups who represent the prosecution are to review the events of the story to find arguments which will convict Henry of desertion.

Give students time to work in their groups to gather their data and make their arguments.

Then have all the prosecutors get together to consolidate their data, organize their arguments, and prepare their case against Henry. Meanwhile, the students for the defense should get together to prepare their case as well.

Students should take most of one class period to prepare their cases. In preparing their cases, students should also prepare their witnesses. Students from each group must play the parts of the various witnesses who are to be called. One person from the group must be the chief prosecutor or defense attorney. You, the teacher, should appoint the person who will be the judge.

Activity #2
While students are preparing their cases, call students to your desk (or some other private area) to discuss their papers from Writing Assignment #1. A Writing Evaluation Form is included with this unit to help structure your conferences.

LESSON TWELVE

Objective
To complete the activities begun in Lesson Eleven

Activity
Give students a few minutes to review their notes and their cases and then actually hold the mini-trial of Henry Fleming. Allow the prosecution to present its case, the defense to present its case, and then allow each side five minutes to present final arguments to the judge.

Give the judge time to deliberate and reach a decision. It would be fun to give a prize to the winning team (prosecution or defense).

WRITING EVALUATION FORM - *The Red Badge of Courage*

Name _____ Date _____

Writing Assignment #1 for the *The Red Badge of Courage* unit   Grade _____

Circle One For Each Item:

Grammar: correct   errors noted on paper

Spelling: correct   errors noted on paper

Punctuation: correct   errors noted on paper

Legibility: excellent   good   fair   poor

Strengths:

Weaknesses:

Comments/Suggestions:

CASE PREPARATION WORKSHEET
The Red Badge of Courage

Case preparation for the (defense) or (prosecution) of Henry Fleming on the charge of desertion.

Best Argument:

Evidence Supporting Best Argument:

Second Argument:

Evidence Supporting Second Argument:

Third Argument:

Evidence Supporting Third Argument:

Fourth Argument:

Evidence Supporting Fourth Argument:

Witnesses:

_____ to be played by _____

_____ to be played by _____

_____ to be played by _____

_____ to be played by _____

_____ to be played by _____

_____ to be played by _____

LESSON THIRTEEN

<u>Objectives</u>
1. To give students the opportunity to practice writing to persuade
2. To give the teacher the opportunity to evaluate students' writing skills
3. To give students a grade for the comprehensive work done in the last two class periods
4. To review the facts and ideas presented in the last two class periods

<u>Activity</u>
Distribute Writing Assignment #2 and discuss the directions in detail. Give students ample time to complete the writing assignment, then collect the papers for grading.

WRITING ASSIGNMENT #2 - *The Red Badge of Courage*

PROMPT

In the last two class periods you have reviewed the main elements of *The Red Badge of Courage* as you prepared a case for either the defense or prosecution of Henry Fleming. Your job now is to use the information you prepared to create a written, persuasive argument for either the defense or prosecution of Henry Fleming.

PREWRITING

Most of your prewriting work has been done already and is located on your Case Preparation Worksheet.

DRAFTING

One way to begin is to look at your Case Preparation Worksheet. On it you have most of the information you need to write this composition. First, are you for the defense or prosecution of Henry Fleming? Make this clear in your opening statement, your introductory paragraph. What do the facts you are about to present show? That is your thesis, your main idea.

After you have written your introductory paragraph, write one paragraph for each of the main arguments you have listed on your worksheet. State your argument (which will be your topic sentence) and then, in the body of the paragraph, give the supporting evidence you have gathered. Repeat this for each of the arguments on your worksheet.

Finally, give your concluding remarks, your final remarks (which for a trial would be addressed to the judge or jury) in a concluding paragraph.

PROMPT

When you finish the rough draft of your paper, ask a student who sits near you to read it. After reading your rough draft, he/she should tell you what he/she liked best about your work, which parts were difficult to understand, and ways in which your work could be improved. Reread your paper considering your critic's comments and make the corrections you think are necessary.

PROOFREADING

Do a final proofreading of your paper double-checking your grammar, spelling, organization, and the clarity of your ideas.

LESSON FOURTEEN

Objectives
1. To bring in some relevant present-day topics for discussion
2. To incorporate the reading of relevant nonfiction

Activity #1
Introduce the idea that the American Civil War ended well over a hundred years ago. Remind students, though, that they heard from people who were in combat in more recent times. Bring up the idea of conflicts in our time--things that are going on now in the world, and ask students to name a few places where there are bloody conflicts going on. Locate these places on a world map for your students. Write down the names of the places on the board. If your students do not have many ideas, tell them about places where there are conflicts.

Activity #2
Divide your class into groups--one group for each place of conflict you have written on the board.

Explain to students that they are to read at least one article (each student reads a different article) about the conflict in the place their group has been assigned. Students should read their article through once and then go back and jot down notes about the most important and interesting parts of the article.

Take students to the library so they can do their reading/research.

LESSON FIFTEEN

Objectives
1. To check students' work from Lesson Fourteen
2. To broaden students' knowledge about current affairs
3. To give students the opportunity to practice public speaking

Activity #1
Have students get together in their groups (assigned in Lesson Fourteen). They should take a few minutes to talk about the information they have gathered. Students should compare and contrast their articles and create a summary of the information they have gathered, explaining, at least in part, the conflict in the place they were assigned.

Activity #2
Ask one spokesperson from each group to give an oral summary of the group's research.

LESSON SIXTEEN

Objectives
    1. To give students practice writing to inform
    2. To give the teacher the opportunity to evaluate students' writing skills
    3. To have students synthesize the information they have gathered for the nonfiction reading assignment

Activity
    Distribute Writing Assignment #3 and discuss the directions in detail. Give students ample time to complete the assignment and then collect the papers for grading.

LESSONS SEVENTEEN AND EIGHTEEN

Objectives
    1. To show one film maker's version of Crane's *Red Badge of Courage*
    2. To give students the opportunity to compare and contrast the film version of the book with the written text and their own visualizations of the story
    3. To put together on screen the whole of all the pieces students have studied during the past sixteen lessons

Activity #1
    Show a film version of *The Red Badge of Courage*.

Activity #2
    After viewing the film, have students compare and contrast the film version of *Red Badge* with the text and their own visualizations of the text.

WRITING ASSIGNMENT #3 - *The Red Badge of Courage*

PROMPT

You have spent two class periods researching and learning about different conflicts in our world today. Now your assignment is to write a composition in which you inform your reader about one of those conflicts.

PREWRITNG

Your prewriting work has been done through your research and group work. Review your notes from those activities. You may write about any conflict you wish; however, it will probably be easiest for you to write about the conflict your researched and discussed in your group.

DRAFTING

One way to begin is to introduce the place you will write about. Let your reader know where it is and what the basic conflict(s) is (are). That information will go in your introductory paragraph.

The contents of the body of your composition will vary depending upon what kind of information you gathered about your place of conflict. In general, the best way to handle your information is to locate the main types of information you have and write one paragraph for each type of information. For example, you may have background information, information about the current status of the conflict, information about leader(s) in the conflict, and/or information about the outlook for this place of conflict. Organize your material in a logical sequence.

PROMPT

When you finish the rough draft of your paper, ask a student who sits near you to read it. After reading your rough draft, he/she should tell you what he/she liked best about your work, which parts were difficult to understand, and ways in which your work could be improved. Reread your paper considering your critic's comments and make the corrections you think are necessary.

PROOFREADING

Do a final proofreading of your paper double-checking your grammar, spelling, organization, and the clarity of your ideas.

LESSON NINETEEN

Objective
       To review the main ideas presented in *The Red Badge of Courage*

Activity #1
       Choose one of the review games/activities included in this unit plan and spend your class period as outlined there. Some materials for these activities are located in the Extra Activities section of this unit.

Activity #2
       Remind students that the Unit Test will be in the next class meeting. Stress the review of the Study Guides and their class notes as a last-minute, brush-up review for homework.

REVIEW GAMES/ACTIVITIES - *The Red Badge of Courage*

1. Ask the class to make up a unit test for *The Red Badge of Courage*. The test should have 4 sections: matching, true/false, short answer, and essay. Students may use 1/2 period to make the test and then swap papers and use the other 1/2 class period to take a test a classmate has devised (open book). You may want to use the unit test included in this section or take questions from the students' unit tests to formulate your own test.

2. Take 1/2 period for students to make up true and false questions (including the answers). Collect the papers and divide the class into two teams. Draw a big tic-tac-toe board on the chalk board. Make one team X and one team O. Ask questions to each side, giving each student one turn. If the question is answered correctly, that students' team's letter (X or O) is placed in the box. If the answer is incorrect, no mark is placed in the box. The object is to get three marks in a row like tic-tac-toe. You may want to keep track of the number of games won for each team.

3. Take 1/2 period for students to make up questions (true/false and short answer). Collect the questions. Divide the class into two teams. You'll alternate asking questions to individual members of teams A & B (like in a spelling bee). The question keeps going from A to B until it is correctly answered, then a new question is asked. A correct answer does not allow the team to get another question. Correct answers are +2 points; incorrect answers are -1 point.

4. Have students pair up and quiz each other from their study guides and class notes.

5. Give students a *The Red Badge of Courage* crossword puzzle to complete.

6. Divide your class into two teams. Use *The Red Badge of Courage* crossword words with their letters jumbled as a word list. Student 1 from Team A faces off against Student 1 from Team B. You write the first jumbled word on the board. The first student (1A or 1B) to unscramble the word wins the chance for his/her team to score points. If 1A wins the jumble, go to student 2A and give him/her a clue. He/she must give you the correct word which matches that clue. If he/she does, Team A scores a point, and you give student 3A a clue for which you expect another correct response. Continue giving Team A clues until some team member makes an incorrect response. An incorrect response sends the game back to the jumbled-word face off, this time with students 2A and 2B. Instead of repeating giving clues to the first few students of each team, continue with the student after the one who gave the last incorrect response on the team. For example, if Team B wins the jumbled-word face-off, and student 5B gave the last incorrect answer for Team B, you would start this round of clue questions with student 6B, and so on. The team with the most points wins!

UNIT TESTS

SHORT ANSWER UNIT TEST #1 - *The Red Badge of Courage*

I. Multiple Choice

___ 1. Tall soldier Jim
    A. Fleming   B. Crane   C. Wilson   D. Conklin

___ 2. Author
    A. Fleming   B. Crane   C. Wilson   D. Henry

___ 3. Soldier Fleming
    A. Jim   B. Wilson   C. Henry   D. Crane

___ 4. Point of view from which the story is written
    A. Omniscient   B. First Person   C. Henry's   D. Personification

___ 5. Giving human characteristics to inhuman things
    A. Omniscient   B. Realism   C. Romanticism   D. Personification

___ 6. Man Henry left in the man's time of need
    A. Tattered Man   B. Wilson   C. Tall soldier   D. Loud Soldier

___ 7. The Loud Soldier
    A. Tattered Man   B. Fleming   C. Wilson   D. Jim

II. Short Answer

1. The youth "wished that he, too, had a wound, a red badge of courage." Why?

2. Henry is finally wounded. By whom and how?

3. What was Henry's lie to Wilson upon his return to the regiment?

Red Badge Short Answer Unit Test 1 Page 2

4. "He had slept and, awakening, had found himself a knight." Explain.

5. What is Henry's "sin"?

6. Give an example from the novel for each of the following:
    a. Man vs. himself

    b. Man vs. nature

    c. Man vs. man

    d. Romantic vs. realistic

    e. Personification

    f. Crane's use of comparison

Red Badge Short Answer Unit Test 1 Page 3

III. In-depth Answer Required (Use the back of this page if necessary.)

1. Describe Henry's character development through the novel.

2. What does Henry decide in his final evaluation of himself?

Red Badge Short Answer Unit Test 1 Page 4

IV. Vocabulary

    Listen to the vocabulary words and write them down. Go back later and write in the correct definitions.

1.

2.

3.

4.

5.

6.

7.

8.

9.

10.

SHORT ANSWER UNIT TEST #2 - *The Red Badge of Courage*

I. Multiple Choice

___ 1. Tall soldier Jim
     A. Wilson   B. Conklin   C. Fleming   D. Crane

___ 2. Author
     A. Crane   B. Fleming   C. Wilson   D. Henry

___ 3. Soldier Fleming
     A. Jim   B. Crane   C. Wilson   D. Henry

___ 4. Point of view from which the story is written
     A. Henry's   B. First Person   C. Omniscient   D. Personification

___ 5. Giving human characteristics to inhuman things
     A. Omniscient   B. Realism   C. Personification   D. Romanticism

___ 6. Man Henry left in the man's time of need
     A. Wilson   B. Tattered Man   C. Tall soldier   D. Loud Soldier

___ 7. The Loud Soldier
     A. Wilson   B. Fleming   C. Tattered Man   D. Jim

II. Short Answer

1. What made Henry feel like a "mental outcast"?

2. Why does Henry think "it would be better to get killed directly"?

3. Why did the squirrel's running make him feel better?

4. What did the tattered man want from Henry? Why did he keep talking to Henry?

Red Badge Short Answer Unit Test 2 Page 2

5. Henry is finally wounded. By whom and how?

6. Why is it significant that Henry asks Wilson where he's going to sleep and what he's going to sleep in?

7. What made Henry "suddenly a modest person"?

8. In the battle in Chapter 22, Henry was "deeply absorbed as a spectator" with "serene self-confidence." Contrast this with his attitude in earlier battles.

Red Badge Short Answer Unit Test 2 Page 3

III. Composition

1. What is the main conflict in *The Red Badge of Courage*?
   Give a <u>complete</u> explanation of your answer.

2. Why did Henry want/need a "red badge of courage"?
   Give a <u>complete</u> explanation in your answer.

KEY: SHORT ANSWER UNIT TESTS - *The Red Badge of Courage*

The short answer questions are taken directly from the study guides.
If you need to look up the answers, you will find them in the study guide section.

Answers to the composition questions will vary depending on your
class discussions and the level of your students.

For the vocabulary section of the test, choose ten of the
words from the vocabulary lists to read orally for your students.

The answers to the matching section of the test are below.

Test #1	Test #2
1. D	1. B
2. B	2. A
3. C	3. D
4. A	4. C
5. D	5. C
6. A	6. B
7. C	7. A

ADVANCED SHORT ANSWER UNIT TEST - *The Red Badge of Courage*

I. Complete answers are required:

1. Describe Henry's development through the book.

2. What was the importance of the Tattered Man?

3. Discuss the use of realism and romanticism in the story.

4. What was the main theme of *Red Badge*? Explain.

5. Explain why the characters have two names--one general and one specific.

Red Badge Advanced Unit Test Page 2

II. Composition

Red Badge describes a couple of days in the life of Henry Fleming. Write a summary of *Red Badge* in which you imitate Stephen Crane's style of writing. Be sure to effectively use descriptive words, active verbs, comparisons, personification, and details.

Red Badge Advanced Unit Test Page 3

III. Vocabulary

> Listen to the vocabulary words and write them down. Go back and write a short composition in which you use all of the vocabulary words given.

MULTIPLE CHOICE UNIT TEST 1 - *The Red Badge of Courage*

I. Multiple Choice

1. What question caused the youthful soldier great concern?
    a. He wondered if he would have enough ammunition.
    b. He wondered if he would run from battle.
    c. He wondered if the officers knew what they were closing.
    d. He wondered if his comrades would leave him alone in battle.

2. From whose point of view is the story written?
    a. Henry's
    b. Omniscient
    c. First Person
    d. A soldier who had been observing

3. What made Henry feel like a "mental outcast"?
    a. He was smarter than everyone else.
    b. He wasn't as smart as everyone else.
    c. He thought no one else was worried about running from battle.
    d. He was the only realist.

4. Why does Henry think "it would be better to get killed directly"?
    a. He would probably be killed eventually, so he might as well get it over with.
    b. He was worried he might have a grotesque, life-long injury.
    c. He hated his life, anyway.
    d. He'd rather be dead than wonder and worry about what will happen.

5. Why did the squirrel's running make him feel better?
    a. Henry was glad to see some creature unaffected by the war.
    b. It helped Henry rationalize his own flight from danger.
    c. He was glad to see that something could run, as he wished he could.
    d. The squirrel was something cute in an otherwise horrid environment.

6. Why didn't the youth want to talk to the tattered man?
    a. Henry didn't want to admit his cowardice.
    b. Henry was hurt too much to talk.
    c. The tattered man gave him the creeps.
    d. He didn't want to witness the tattered man's death.

Red Badge Multiple Choice Test 1 Page 2

7. What did the tattered man want from Henry?
    a. Henry never found out what he wanted.
    b. A promise that he would not let him die in the road
    c. Companionship
    d. His personal papers returned

8. How is Henry wounded?
    a. Henry is shot in the head.
    b. A bullet just grazes Henry's head.
    c. Henry runs into a tree and hurts his head.
    d. A soldier hits Henry in the head with his rifle.

9. "And they were men." Explain.
    a. There were no women in their regiment.
    b. The youthful regiment had seen war and grown older and wiser.
    c. By the time of this battle, all the boys had had their 18th birthday.
    d. b and c

10. Henry evaluates himself. What does he decide?
    a. His public deeds in battle were good.
    b. His treatment of the tattered soldier was justifiable and okay.
    c. He still wishes he had been killed early on in the fighting.
    d. His life isn't worth living because of his shameful retreat and his unkind treatment of the tattered soldier.

Red Badge Multiple Choice Test 1 Page 3

II. Multiple Choice 2

1. Henry should not shirk his duty because of
   - A. mother
   - B. Wilson
   - C. Conklin
   - D. conscience

2. Henry thought it would be better to get _____ directly
   - A. courage
   - B. outcast
   - C. water
   - D. killed

3. Author Stephen
   - A. Conklin
   - B. Fleming
   - C. Crane
   - D. Wilson

4. He had slept and awakening had found himself _____
   - A. alone
   - B. captured
   - C. cold
   - D. a knight

5. Henry felt like an _____
   - A. idiot
   - B. officer
   - C. outcast
   - D. enemy

6. Soldier Fleming
   - A. Stephen
   - B. Jim
   - C. Wilson
   - D. Henry

7. Henry's first concern was that he would _____ battle
   - A. die in
   - B. run from
   - C. be too far from
   - D. like

8. Henry endowed the flag with this because no harm could come to it.
   - A. wisdom
   - B. power
   - C. life
   - D. hope

9. Henry wished he were _____, so he wouldn't have to face his embarrassing retreat
   - A. home
   - B. alone
   - C. dead
   - D. omniscient

10. Seeing things as they really are
    - A. realistic
    - B. romantic
    - C. personification
    - D. omniscient

11. The officers neglected to stand in _____ attitudes
    - A. omniscient
    - B. realistic
    - C. romantic
    - D. picturesque

Red Badge Multiple Choice Test 1 Page 4

III. Quotations
    Explain the significance of each of these quotations:

1. "Apparently the other [Wilson] had now climbed a peak of wisdom from which he could perceive himself a very wee thing."

2. "He [Henry] had been taught that many obligations in life were easily avoided."

3. "Well, don't we fight like the devil . . . . ?"

4. "He had slept and, awakening, had found himself a knight."

5. "The retreat of the mule drivers was a march of shame to him. . . . He presently wrapped his heart in a cloak of pride and kept the flag erect."

Red Badge Multiple Choice Test 1 Page 5

IV. Vocabulary

___ 1. Impetus   A. outwardly calm or composed; complacent

___ 2. Sinuous   B. enormous, extraordinary; marvelous

___ 3. Malediction   C. a curse or slander

___ 4. Blithe   D. portentous; foreboding

___ 5. Interminable   E. endless

___ 6. Vindication   F. impelling force; impulse; stimulus

___ 7. Perfunctory   G. made wet and limp

___ 8. Sullen   H. morose, sulky

___ 9. Impending   I. reprimand

___ 10. Heedless   J. acting with little interest or care

___ 11. Ominous   K. arousing fear or dread; awesome; difficult to overtake

___ 12. Prodigious   L. paying little or no attention; unmindful

___ 13. Delirium   M. likely to happen soon

___ 14. Specter   N. the evidence or argument that justifies an act

___ 15. Formidable   O. ghost; phantasm

___ 16. Bedraggled   P. cheerful; casual; carefree

___ 17. Reproof   Q. the act of coming down voluntarily to the level of inferiors

___ 18. Facetious   R. temporary mental confusion

___ 19. Condescension S. humorous and flippant; playfully jocular

___ 20. Placidly   T. winding

MULTIPLE CHOICE UNIT TEST 2 - *The Red Badge of Courage*

I. Multiple Choice
1. What question caused the youthful soldier great concern?
    a. He wondered if he would have enough ammunition.
    b. He wondered if the officers knew what they were doing.
    c. He wondered if he would run from battle.
    d. He wondered if his comrades would leave him alone in battle.

2. From whose point of view is the story written?
    a. Omniscient
    b. Henry's
    c. First Person
    d. A soldier who had been observing

3. What made Henry feel like a "mental outcast"?
    a. He was smarter than everyone else.
    b. He wasn't as smart as everyone else.
    c. He was the only realist.
    d. He thought no one else was worried about running from battle.

4. Why does Henry think "it would be better to get killed directly"?
    a. He'd rather be dead than wonder and worry about what will happen.
    b. He was worried he might have a grotesque, life-long injury.
    c. He hated his life, anyway.
    d. He would probably be killed eventually, so he might as well get it over with.

5. Why did the squirrel's running make him feel better?
    a. Henry was glad to see some creature unaffected by the war.
    b. The squirrel was something cute in an otherwise horrid environment.
    c. He was glad to see that something could run, as he wished he could.
    d. It helped Henry rationalize his own flight from danger.

6. Why didn't the youth want to talk to the tattered man?
    a. Henry was hurt too much to talk.
    b. Henry didn't want to admit his cowardice.
    c. The tattered man gave him the creeps.
    d. He didn't want to witness the tattered man's death.

Red Badge Multiple Choice Unit Test 2 Page 2

7. What did the tattered man want from Henry?
    a. Henry never found out what he wanted.
    b. A promise that he would not let him die in the road
    c. His personal papers returned
    d. Companionship

8. How was Henry wounded?
    a. Henry was shot in the head.
    b. A bullet just grazed Henry's head.
    c. Henry ran into a tree and hurt his head.
    d. A soldier hit Henry in the head with his rifle.

9. This chapter ends with "And they were men." Explain.
    a. There were no women in their regiment.
    b. They were no longer a green, youthful regiment; they had seen war and grown older and wiser.
    c. By the time of this battle, all the boys had had their 18th birthday.
    d. b and c

10. In this chapter, Henry evaluates himself. What does he decide?
    a. His public deeds in battle were good.
    b. His treatment of the tattered soldier was justifiable and okay.
    c. He still wishes he had been killed early on in the fighting.
    d. His life isn't worth living because of his shameful retreat and his unkind treatment of the tattered soldier.

Red Badge Multiple Choice Unit Test 2 Page 3

II. Multiple Choice 2

1. Henry should not shirk his duty because of
   A. conscience B. Wilson C. Conklin D. mother

2. Henry thought it would be better to get _____ directly
   A. killed B. outcast C. water D. courage

3. Author Stephen
   A. Conklin B. Crane C. Fleming D. Wilson

4. He had slept and awakening had found himself _____
   A. alone B. captured C. a knight D. cold

5. Henry felt like an _____
   A. outcast B. officer C. idiot D. enemy

6. Soldier Fleming
   A. Stephen B. Jim C. Wilson D. Henry

7. Henry's first concern was that he would _____ battle
   A. die in B. be too far from C. run from D. like

8. Henry endowed the flag with this because no harm could come to it.
   A. wisdom B. hope C. life D. power

9. Henry wished he were _____, so he wouldn't have to face his embarrassing retreat
   A. home B. alone C. dead D. omniscient

10. Seeing things as they really are
    A. realistic B. romantic C. personification D. omniscient

11. The officers neglected to stand in _____ attitudes
    A. omniscient B. picturesque C. romantic D. realistic

Red Badge Multiple Choice Unit Test 2 Page 4

III. Quotations
    Explain the significance of each of the following quotations:

1. No one seemed to be wrestling with such a terrific personal problem. He was a mental outcast.

2. There was a singular absence of heroic poses.

3. "Apparently the other [Wilson] had now climbed a peak of wisdom from which he could perceive himself a very wee thing."

4. "He [Henry] had been taught that many obligations in life were easily avoided."

5. "Well, don't we fight like the devil . . . . ?"

6. "The retreat of the mule drivers was a march of shame to him. . . . He presently wrapped his heart in a cloak of pride and kept the flag erect."

Red Badge Multiple Choice Unit Test 2 Page 5

IV. Vocabulary

___ 1. Specter   a. portentous; foreboding

___ 2. Ominous   b. wiped out; destroyed completely

___ 3. Ponderous   c. broken down; falling apart; ruined

___ 4. Ludicrous   d. continually

___ 5. Denoted   e. an open condemnation or censure

___ 6. Indignantly   f. feeling disheartened or dejected

___ 7. Disconcerted   g. ghost; phantasm

___ 8. Sardonic   h. a recurrent chill or fit of shivering

___ 9. Discerned   i. laughable because of obvious absurdity or incongruity

___ 10. Malediction   j. lacking self-composure

___ 11. Despondent   k. marked; indicated; signified

___ 12. Denunciation   l. massive

___ 13. Exasperation   m. with an anger aroused by something unjust

___ 14. Formidable   n. arousing fear or dread; awesome; Difficult to overtake

___ 15. Annihilated   o. fearless; bold

___ 16. Vindication   p. the state of extremely annoyed or irritated

___ 17. Ague   q. the evidence or argument that justifies an act

___ 18. Dauntless   r. detected; perceived

___ 19. Perpetually   s. mocking; cynical

___ 20. Dilapidated   t. a curse or slander

ANSWER SHEET FOR MULTIPLE CHOICE UNIT TESTS
The Red Badge of Courage

I. Multiple Choice
1. (A) (B) (C) (D)
2. (A) (B) (C) (D)
3. (A) (B) (C) (D)
4. (A) (B) (C) (D)
5. (A) (B) (C) (D)
6. (A) (B) (C) (D)
7. (A) (B) (C) (D)
8. (A) (B) (C) (D)
9. (A) (B) (C) (D)
10. (A) (B) (C) (D)

II. Multiple Choice 2
1. (A) (B) (C) (D)
2. (A) (B) (C) (D)
3. (A) (B) (C) (D)
4. (A) (B) (C) (D)
5. (A) (B) (C) (D)
6. (A) (B) (C) (D)
7. (A) (B) (C) (D)
8. (A) (B) (C) (D)
9. (A) (B) (C) (D)
10. (A) (B) (C) (D)
11. (A) (B) (C) (D)

III. Vocabulary
1. ___
2. ___
3. ___
4. ___
5. ___
6. ___
7. ___
8. ___
9. ___
10. ___
11. ___
12. ___
13. ___
14. ___
15. ___
16. ___
17. ___
18. ___
19. ___
20. ___

ANSWER KEY FOR MULTIPLE CHOICE UNIT TEST 1
The Red Badge of Courage

I. Multiple Choice	II. Multiple Choice 2	III. Vocabulary	
1. (A) ( ) (C) (D)	1. ( ) (B) (C) (D)	1.	F
2. (A) ( ) (C) (D)	2. (A) (B) (C) ( )	2.	T
3. (A) (B) ( ) (D)	3. (A) (B) ( ) (D)	3.	C
4. (A) (B) (C) ( )	4. (A) (B) (C) ( )	4.	P
5. (A) ( ) (C) (D)	5. (A) (B) ( ) (D)	5.	E
6. ( ) (B) (C) (D)	6. (A) (B) (C) ( )	6.	N
7. (A) (B) ( ) (D)	7. (A) ( ) (C) (D)	7.	J
8. (A) (B) (C) ( )	8. (A) ( ) (C) (D)	8.	H
9. (A) ( ) (C) (D)	9. (A) (B) ( ) (D)	9.	M
10. ( ) (B) (C) (D)	10. ( ) (B) (C) (D)	10.	L
	11. (A) (B) (C) ( )	11.	D
		12.	B
		13.	R
		14.	O
		15.	K
		16.	G
		17.	I
		18.	S
		19.	Q
		20.	A

ANSWER KEY FOR MULTIPLE CHOICE UNIT TEST 2
The Red Badge of Courage

I. Multiple Choice
1. (A) (B) ( ) (D)
2. ( ) (B) (C) (D)
3. (A) (B) (C) ( )
4. ( ) (B) (C) (D)
5. (A) (B) (C) ( )
6. (A) ( ) (C) (D)
7. (A) (B) (C) ( )
8. (A) (B) (C) ( )
9. (A) ( ) (C) (D)
10. ( ) (B) (C) (D)

II. Multiple Choice 2
1. (A) (B) (C) ( )
2. ( ) (B) (C) (D)
3. (A) ( ) (C) (D)
4. (A) (B) ( ) (D)
5. ( ) (B) (C) (D)
6. (A) (B) (C) ( )
7. (A) (B) ( ) (D)
8. (A) (B) (C) ( )
9. (A) (B) ( ) (D)
10. ( ) (B) (C) (D)
11. (A) ( ) (C) (D)

III. Vocabulary
1. G
2. A
3. L
4. I
5. K
6. M
7. J
8. S
9. R
10. T
11. F
12. E
13. P
14. N
15. B
16. Q
17. H
18. O
19. D
20. C

UNIT RESOURCE MATERIALS

BULLETIN BOARD IDEAS - *The Red Badge of Courage*

1. Save one corner of the board for the best of students' *The Red Badge of Courage* writing assignments.

2. Check your school or public library for pictures from the Civil War. Post them on colorful paper on your board.

3. Title the board PAINTING AN IMAGE: THE RED BADGE OF COURAGE. Write out the passage from chapter 4 on the board. After Lesson Four -- or as you review the "answers" to the lesson, use different colored markers to highlight nouns, adjectives, descriptive words, active verbs, personification, and comparisons. On one corner of the board key the colors to what they represent.

4. Take one of the word search puzzles from the extra activities section and with a marker copy it over in a large size on the bulletin board. Write the clue words to find to one side. Invite students prior to and after class to find the words and circle them on the bulletin board.

5. Throughout the unit have students bring in articles about conflicts/wars which are currently happening in the world. Post the articles on the bulletin board. (Perhaps offer some kind of extra credit or special prize for those students who have articles put on the board.)

6. Title the board HOW DO YOU KNOW WHEN YOU'RE GROWN UP? Have students bring in pictures of things that answer that question and post them on the board. This would also make a good introductory activity.

7. Write several of the most significant quotations from the book on the board on brightly colored paper.

8. Do a bulletin board about the armed services--career opportunities in the army, navy, air force, marines, coast guard, etc.

9. Make a bulletin board listing the vocabulary words for this unit. As you complete sections of the novel and discuss the vocabulary for each section, write the definitions on the bulletin board. (If your board is one students face frequently, it will help them learn the words.)

EXTRA ACTIVITIES

One of the difficulties in teaching a novel is that all students don't read at the same speed. One student who likes to read may take the book home and finish it in a day or two. Sometimes a few students finish the in-class assignments early. The problem, then, is finding suitable extra activities for students.

The best thing I've found is to keep a little library in the classroom. For this unit on *The Red Badge of Courage*, you might check out from the school library other books by Stephen Crane. A biography of Crane would be interesting for some students. You can include other related books and articles about the Civil War, general history of the period, and perhaps other books by some other American realists.

The other things you may keep on hand are word search puzzles. We have made some of them relating directly to *The Red Badge of Courage* for you. Feel free to duplicate them.

Some students may like to draw. You might devise a contest or allow some extra-credit grade for students who draw characters or scenes from *The Red Badge of Courage*. Note, too, that if the students do not want to keep their drawings you may pick up some extra bulletin board materials this way. If you have a contest and you supply the prize (a CD or something like that perhaps), you could, possibly, make the drawing itself a non-refundable entry fee.

MORE ACTIVITIES - *The Red Badge of Courage*

1. Compare and contrast Crane's writing style with another American author's. (Teacher's note: You may wish to choose an author or a group of authors with which your class would be familiar.)

2. Choose one scene from *Red Badge* and write it as a play. Then explain the difficulties, if any, you encountered in doing so.

3. There are many letters and accounts of battles written by participants in the Civil War. Find one such account and write a summary of it, comparing it (when possible) to *The Red Badge of Courage*.

4. Pretend you are Henry at the end of the story and write a letter to your mother about your recent adventures.

5. Write and title the next chapter (following the end) of *Red Badge* as you think it would happen.

6. Research and write a report about one battle of the Civil War. (Teacher's note: Perhaps you would assign different battles to each student so everyone doesn't end up doing all the same battle, causing a shortage of resources on the topic.)

7. Have students design a book cover (front and back and inside flaps) for *The Red Badge of Courage*.

8. Have students design a bulletin board (ready to be put up, not just sketched) for *The Red Badge of Courage*.

9. Use some of the related topics (noted earlier for an in-class library) as topics for research, reports, or written papers, or as topics for guest speakers.

10. Divide the class into two groups--North and South. Have each side research and report on its views for the war, uniforms and weapons, successes and failures during the war, and other relevant topics. Perhaps they could construct uniforms, flags, maps and other props which would make reports more interesting. Also, I suggest that each student in the group be given one topic to research. That way, everyone has something specific to be responsible for.

11. Have students work together to construct a map of Henry's travels through the novel.

12. Most areas of the U.S. have local groups of people who are Civil War buffs, people who study the war as a hobby or profession. Some areas also have groups of men who actually reenact battles from the war. Seek out these people in your area. Check with your local chamber of commerce or historical society to find out how to contact the people in your area. The librarian at your public library might also be able to help you locate people who have an interest in the Civil War. Prior to beginning this unit you might also ask your students if they know anyone who is a Civil War buff.

Once you have located these people, have them dress in the appropriate uniform(s). At least try to borrow uniform costumes or have samples of swords, bayonets, or guns used during the war.

Have the Civil War buffs take sides--some for the North and some for the South. Put them into a verbal debate about why they were fighting and who won and why. Rather than just making this a lecture from one person, try to get at least two people to interact discussing the war from two different points of view and let your students observe. Then allow time for specific questions from your students.

WORD SEARCH - *The Red Badge of Courage*

All words in this list are associated with *The Red Badge of Courage*. The words are placed backwards, forward, diagonally, up and down. The included words are listed below the word search.

```
Z C Q T X T F H F T Z B V G N N J Z S S V P N B
J M Q L L Q L C T B M W S P I B H Q H P S P P G
Y V Z V N E X W K P D Q M L G T U P Z W S Q K H
Q Q D W Z C P T V I P Z K S Y I V K A Z S H Y P
N L R O J K N A Z L L N C N R Q T T C L F R F J
H L R V R K R L H K O L H R U E E J R T G E F D
V E U Q S E R U T C I P E N A R C B A D G E A L
H F N N T Z D T O K I L N D D O G I N D K E T R
D W L R K W C R Z H F T K F U Y C U F O D H H F
C T E A Y H P T O I E T N R B R O R M F T D D N
A A G P G S E R R M C T A A D W E S F W O F O E
T R F W E K T A A M N G Q T M H H A Y O A S W D
F V T V C P Z H D E E I G B T O C M L M R N H
D Y Z I V Q S G M S G K S O T E R B J I B I G Q
Y J H J L T H I P C D M M C Z M R B W K S O P P
T T G L H L G S V Y G L J P I B W E A N S T L H
D R P G J E E J Y N G Z L Y O E H K D T J S I C
T H I K R G D R O U T C A S T W N K D J T H N C
W N N K M H K W Y V P K Q R W N E T S C K L B R
K W D L P N O I T A C I F I N O S R E P C R E B
```

ARTILLERY	FLAG	OUTCAST	SHOT
BADGE	FOE	PERSONIFICATION	SIN
BATTLE	HENRY	PICTURESQUE	SMOKE
BLOOD	HERO	POWER	SQUIRREL
CHAPEL	KILLED	REALISTIC	SYMBOL
CONKLIN	KNIGHT	REGIMENT	TATTERED
CORPSE	LUNKHEADS	RETREAT	THICKET
COURAGE	MOTHER	RIFLE	WAR
CRANE	OFFICERS	ROMANTIC	WATER
DEAD	OMNISCIENT	RUN	WILSON
FEAR	ORDER	SHAME	WOUND

CROSSWORD - *The Red Badge of Courage*

CROSSWORD CLUES - *The Red Badge of Courage*

ACROSS

1. Injury; where a bullet may have hit for example
2. Red fluid on soldiers' bandages
6. Place in forest where Henry came upon the dead soldier
7. Henry lies about his wound and says he was _____.
11. Henry's _____ was deserting the tattered soldier
12. Seeing things as they really are; not romantic
14. Soldier Fleming
16. Point of view from which the story is written
18. One others exalt because of his deeds
19. Enemy
22. Firing gunpowder caused this, which made seeing difficult
24. Command soldiers follow
26. Man Henry left in the man's time of need
27. Military unit consisting of Battalions, et al.
28. They give commands

DOWN

1. The loud soldier
2. Red _____ of Courage
3. An episode of fighting
4. Henry wished he were _____, so he wouldn't have to face his embarrassing retreat
5. Henry should not shirk his duty because of her
6. Tall soldier Jim
8. Henry carried it into battle
9. Long gun
10. He had slept and awakening had found himself a _____
11. Something that stands for something else
12. Unrealistic; seeing things rosier than they really are
13. Henry threw a pine cone at one, and it ran away
15. The officers neglected to stand in _____ attitudes
17. The retreat of the mule drivers was a march of _____ to Henry
19. Feeling of being afraid
20. Henry endowed the flag with this because no harm could come to it.
21. Liquid in soldiers' canteens
23. Dead body
25. Henry's first concern was that he would _____ from battle.

CROSSWORD ANSWER KEY - *The Red Badge of Courage*

MATCHING QUIZ/WORKSHEET 1 - *The Red Badge of Courage*

___ 1. OMNISCIENT   A. He had slept and awakening had found himself a _____

___ 2. THICKET   B. They give commands

___ 3. PICTURESQUE   C. Long gun

___ 4. CONKLIN   D. Injury; where a bullet may have hit for example

___ 5. PERSONIFICATION   E. Giving human characteristics to inhuman things

___ 6. WOUND   F. Henry wished he were _____, so he wouldn't have to face his embarrassing retreat

___ 7. RUN   G. Place in forest where Henry came upon the dead soldier

___ 8. ROMANTIC   H. Henry's _____ was deserting the tattered soldier

___ 9. WATER   I. Bravery

___ 10. OFFICERS   J. What the soldiers called their inept commanders

___ 11. MOTHER   K. Unrealistic; seeing things rosier than they really are

___ 12. RIFLE   L. The officers neglected to stand in ___ attitudes

___ 13. SIN   M. Tall soldier Jim

___ 14. DEAD   N. The retreat of the mule drivers was a march of _____ to Henry

___ 15. LUNKHEADS   O. Dense growth of shrubs and underbrush

___ 16. CHAPEL   P. Liquid in soldiers' canteens

___ 17. TATTERED   Q. Henry's first concern was that he would _____ from battle

___ 18. KNIGHT   R. Henry should not shirk his duty because of her

___ 19. COURAGE   S. Man Henry left in the man's time of need

___ 20. SHAME   T. Point of view from which they story is written

MATCHING QUIZ/WORKSHEET 2 - *The Red Badge of Courage*

___ 1. HENRY   A. Place in forest where Henry came upon the dead soldier

___ 2. CRANE   B. Injury; where a bullet may have hit for example

___ 3. BADGE   C. What the soldiers called their inept commanders

___ 4. WOUND   D. Red _____ of Courage

___ 5. WAR   E. The Civil _____

___ 6. CHAPEL   F. Henry felt like a mental _____

___ 7. KNIGHT   G. Giving human characteristics to inhuman things

___ 8. CONKLIN   H. They give commands

___ 9. CORPSE   I. Dead body

___ 10. REGIMENT   J. Feeling of being afraid

___ 11. OFFICERS   K. Enemy

___ 12. PERSONIFICATION   L. Red fluid on soldiers' bandages

___ 13. OUTCAST   M. Tall soldier Jim

___ 14. DEAD   N. Soldier Fleming

___ 15. TATTERED   O. Long gun

___ 16. RIFLE   P. Military unit consisting of Battalions, et al.

___ 17. FEAR   Q. Author Stephen

___ 18. LUNKHEADS   R. He had slept and awakening had found himself a _____

___ 19. FOE   S. Man Henry left in the man's time of need

___ 20. BLOOD   T. Henry wished he were _____, so he wouldn't have to face his embarrassing retreat

KEYS: MATCHING QUIZ/WORKSHEETS - *The Red Badge of Courage*

Worksheet 1	Worksheet 2
1. T	1. N
2. O	2. Q
3. L	3. D
4. M	4. B
5. E	5. E
6. D	6. A
7. Q	7. R
8. K	8. M
9. P	9. I
10. B	10. P
11. R	11. H
12. C	12. G
13. H	13. F
14. F	14. T
15. J	15. S
16. G	16. O
17. S	17. J
18. A	18. C
19. I	19. K
20. N	20. L

JUGGLE LETTER REVIEW GAME CLUE SHEET - *The Red Badge of Courage*

SCRAMBLED	WORD	CLUE
RAECN	CRANE	Author Stephen
RISFECFO	OFFICERS	They give commands
EDDA	DEAD	Henry wished he were _____, so he wouldn't have to face his embarrassing retreat
AFRE	FEAR	Feeling of being afraid
OEF	FOE	Enemy
GAFL	FLAG	Henry carried it into battle
IRCSAELTI	REALISTIC	Seeing things as they really are; not romantic
LBOYMS	SYMBOL	Something that stands for something else
IIENMSNOTC	OMNISCIENT	Point of view from which the story is written
RTAWE	WATER	Liquid in soldiers' canteens
SOTTUCA	OUTCAST	Henry felt like a mental outcast
KEMOS	SMOKE	Firing gunpowder
INS	SIN	Henry's _____ was deserting the tattered soldier
RWA	WAR	The Civil _____
IESRURLQ	SQUIRREL	Henry threw a pine cone at one, and it ran away
ILCNONK	CONKLIN	Tall soldier Jim
EGADB	BADGE	Red _____ of Courage
EPRWO	POWER	Henry endowed the flag with this because no harm could come to it
MGETNIER	REGIMENT	Military unit consisting of Battalions, et al.
ETBLTA	BATTLE	An episode of fighting
ORHE	HERO	One others exalt because of his deeds
PCESOR	CORPSE	Dead body
ALDESHUNK	LUNKHEADS	What the soldiers called their inept commanders
EUROGAC	COURAGE	Bravery
TOSH	SHOT	Henry lies about his wound and says he was _____
NLSOIW	WILSON	The loud soldier
UEQRTPIECSU	PICTURESQUE	The officers neglected to stand in _____ attitudes
NHYER	HENRY	Soldier Fleming
REHTMO	MOTHER	Henry should not shirk his duty because of her
IRLYLERTA	ARTILLERY	The big guns; cannons, for example
OOLDB	BLOOD	Red fluid on soldiers' bandages
NRAICMTO	ROMANTIC	Unrealistic; seeing things rosier than they really are
EMSHA	SHAME	The retreat of the mule drivers was a march of ___ to Henry
EERTRTA	RETREAT	Go backward; lose ground in battle
OREPW	POWER	Henry endowed the flag with this because no harm could come to it
DUNWO	WOUND	Injury; where a bullet may have hit for example
APHELC	CHAPEL	Place in forest where Henry came upon the dead soldier
YNREH	HENRY	Soldier Fleming
TSAUCTO	OUTCAST	Henry felt like a mental _____.
OSMEK	SMOKE	Firing gunpowder caused this, which made seeing it difficult

VOCABULARY RESOURCE MATERIALS

VOCABULARY WORD SEARCH - *The Red Badge of Courage*

All words in this list are associated with *The Red Badge of Courage* with emphasis on the vocabulary words from the story. The words are placed backwards, forward, diagonally, up and down. The included words are listed below the word search.

```
V A N Q U I S H E D A E L A T I O N Y C H A O S
P I O B L I G E D L S S C C O D M T K M X D H S
Q D N K R Q D R T O N D E N S B I P Z L L F G Y
K G I D K Y G E P O E J P N A M S S E L D E E H
W B P L I Y R E I T B S O E I I M C C N D S M Q
V Y B Z A C R T A A P I O X R I L E U E D W T Z
M X B T A P A L P R T E O R T P N E N R R I H R
T U V T H C I T O C L R N T O R E U R A I N N L
M H I K E H P D I B P F E J D M N T H Q C T E G
D O P R I K I D A O X N T E W C S I U N Y I Y D
N N P N I G E N S T N N T O I N Q A M A H P N N
J M N F I L I S K F E R B A O P U V F P L N L G
I A R O A M E J T D E D T I O D V Z S A E L S Y
F D U M R L T D N C U I T N A N S A C F X T Y S
H S V E T E R O N R O R D C N P R I O K W Y U L
N Y T N H S P O A N O E I E E D D O N L M O W S
F N U T T S C T S T R O L C O L R H V U N F T V
I A I J E S E B N O U L T N Y P Z B N I O T V K
D L U D I C R O U S U E I T E C A F M A G U E F
B K X D R O C S T S R C Y R D E N O T E D H S H
```

ABJECT	DESPONDENT	MALEDICTION	PROXIMITY
AGUE	DILAPIDATED	MENACING	RELIANCE
ALTERCATION	DISCERNED	MOROSE	REPOSE
ANNIHILATED	DISCONCERTED	OBDURATE	REPROOF
AUDACIOUS	ELATION	OBLIGED	SARDONIC
BLITHE	FACETIOUS	OBSCURITY	SINUOUS
CHAOS	HEEDLESS	OMINOUS	SMITTEN
CONTORTIONS	IMPENDING	ORBS	SPECTER
DAUNTLESS	IMPETUS	PERPETUALLY	SULLEN
DELIRIUM	IMPRECATIONS	PLACIDLY	VANQUISHED
DENOTED	INTERMINABLE	PONDEROUS	VINDICATION
DENUNCIATION	LUDICROUS	PRODIGIOUS	

VOCABULARY CROSSWORD - *The Red Badge of Courage*

VOCABULARY CROSSWORD CLUES - *The Red Badge of Courage*

ACROSS
1. Wiped out; destroyed completely
5. Location; setting
7. Speak to; talk to
10. Broken down; falling apart; ruined
12. Part of a uniform that goes on one's head
13. Wretched; of the most contemptible kind
14. Rest
17. Soldier Fleming
18. Singular; alone
19. Extreme dislike
20. Clothing; garments
22. Body and ----; part of body that may go to an afterlife
23. Cheerful; casual; carefree
24. Enemy
26. Good; pleasant; likable
27. Marked; indicated; signified
29. Unhappy
31. Fearless; bold
32. Outwardly calm or composed; complacent
34. At this moment
36. Henry wished he were _____, so he wouldn't have to face his embarrassing retreat
38. ---- *Badge of Courage*
39. Trudge; walk
41. Portentous; foreboding
42. Melancholy; gloomy; ill-humored
43. Number of fingers on two hands
44. Mocking; cynical
45. Winding

DOWN
1. Heating or noisy quarrel
2. Paying little or no attention; unmindful
3. Laughable because of obvious absurdity or incongruity
4. Exalted feeling arising from a sense of triumph, power or relief
6. Total disorder or confusion
8. Detected; perceived
9. Made wet and limp
11. Arrogantly insolent
13. A recurrent chill or fit of shivering
15. Acting with little interest or care
16. The state of extremely annoyed or irritated
21. Intractable; not giving in
25. Feeling disheartened or dejected
27. Temporary mental confusion
28. The condition of being unknown
30. Humorous and flippant; playfully jocular
33. Impelling force; impulse; stimulus
35. Reprimand
37. Contraction for 'do not'
40. Extend one's hand out for something
41. Eyes
42. Opposite of less

VOCABULARY CROSSWORD ANSWER KEY - *The Red Badge of Courage*

			A	N	N	I	H	I	L	A	T	E	D				P	L	A	C	E
T	E	L	L			E		U		L		D			B				H		
			T			E	D	I	L	A	P	I	D	A	T	E	D		H	A	T
A	B	J	E	C	T		D		I		T		S		U		D			O	
G		R				L		C		I		C		D		R	E	P	O	S	E
U		C		H	E	N	R	Y		O	N	E		A		A		E			X
E	H	A	T	E		S		O		N		R		C		G	A	R	B		A
	O		T			S	O	U	L			N		I		G		F			S
	B	L	I	T	H	E		S		F	O	E		O		L		U			P
	D	O						D				D	U	E		N	I	C	E		
	U	N		D	E	N	O	T	E	D			S	A	D		C				R
	R			E		B		S		F						T					A
D	A	U	N	T	L	E	S	S		P	L	A	C	I	D	L	Y		N	O	W
	T			I		C		O		C		M			R		R				I
D	E	A	D		R		U		N		E		P		E		Y				O
			O		I		R	E	D		T	R	E	K		P			R		N
O	M	I	N	O	U	S		I		E		I		T		M	O	R	O	S	E
R		T		M		T	E	N		O		U		O		O			A		
B						Y		T		U		S	A	R	D	O	N	I	C		
S	I	N	U	O	U	S				S				E		F			H		

VOCABULARY WORKSHEET 1 - *The Red Badge of Courage*

___ 1. SULLEN   A. Exalted feeling arising from a sense of triumph, power or relief

___ 2. VINDICATION   B. Afflicted

___ 3. OBSCURITY   C. Marked; indicated; signified

___ 4. PRODIGIOUS   D. Humorous and flippant; playfully jocular

___ 5. PONDEROUS   E. Threatening

___ 6. MENACING   F. Morose, sulky

___ 7. ALTERCATION   G. Massive

___ 8. EXASPERATION   H. Detected; perceived

___ 9. SMITTEN   I. Endless

___ 10. MOROSE   J. Impelling force; impulse; stimulus

___ 11. RELIANCE   K. Heated or noisy quarrel

___ 12. DENOTED   L. Enormous, extraordinary; marvelous

___ 13. IMPETUS   M. The state of extremely annoyed or irritated

___ 14. FACETIOUS   N. Closeness

___ 15. INTERMINABLE   O. Melancholy; gloomy; ill-humored

___ 16. DISCERNED   P. Confidence; dependence; trust

___ 17. OBLIGED   Q. The evidence or argument that justifies an act

___ 18. PROXIMITY   R. The condition of being unknown

___ 19. DESPONDENT   S. Caused to do something

___ 20. ELATION   T. Feeling disheartened or dejected

VOCABULARY WORKSHEET 2 - *The Red Badge of Courage*

___ 1. Heated or noisy quarrel
    A. repose   B. proximity   C. altercation   D. facetious

___ 2. Acting with little interest or care
    A. interminable   B. sardonic   C. altercation   D. perfunctory

___ 3. Having lacking self-composure
    A. ponderous   B. exasperation   C. specter   D. disconcerted

___ 4. A recurrent chill or fit of shivering
    A. ague   B. annihilated   C. discerned   D. abject

___ 5. Morose, sulky
    A. dauntless   B. sullen   C. indignantly   D. obliged

___ 6. The evidence or argument that justifies an act
    A. ponderous   B. vindication   C. ague   D. altercation

___ 7. Intractable; not giving in
    A. obdurate   B. sinuous   C. interminable   D. denunciation

___ 8. Ghost; phantasm
    A. audacious   B. specter   C. formidable   D. bedraggled

___ 9. Made wet and limp
    A. heedless   B. bedraggled   C. indignantly   D. orbs

___ 10. Cheerful; casual; carefree
    A. dilapidated   B. orbs   C. blithe   D. contortions

___ 11. Massive
    A. disconcerted   B. interminable   C. heedless   D. ponderous

___ 12. Fearless; bold
    A. dauntless   B. prodigious   C. vindication   D. perfunctory

___ 13. Impelling force; impulse; stimulus
    A. repose   B. discerned   C. impetus   D. obscurity

___ 14. Closeness
    A. proximity   B. vanquished   C. denoted   D. sullen

___ 15. Portentous; foreboding
    A. perfunctory   B. sardonic   C. ominous   D. heedless

___ 16. Winding
    A. reproof   B. sinuous   C. interminable   D. sullen

___ 17. Humorous and flippant; playfully jocular
    A. vindication   B. prodigious   C. sullen   D. facetious

___ 18. Broken down; falling apart; ruined
    A. obliged   B. contortions   C. dilapidated   D. menacing

___ 19. Curses
    A. dauntless   B. sinuous   C. ludicrous   D. imprecations

___ 20. Total disorder or confusion
    A. chaos   B. heedless   C. perfunctory   D. menacing

KEY: VOCABULARY WORKSHEETS - *The Red Badge of Courage*

Worksheet 1	Worksheet 2
1. F	1. B
2. Q	2. C
3. R	3. D
4. L	4. A
5. G	5. D
6. E	6. B
7. K	7. A
8. M	8. B
9. B	9. C
10. O	10. C
11. P	11. B
12. C	12. A
13. J	13. C
14. D	14. A
15. I	15. B
16. H	16. B
17. S	17. B
18. N	18. D
19. T	19. C
20. A	20. A

VOCABULARY JUGGLE LETTER REVIEW GAME CLUES - *The Red Badge of Courage*

SCRAMBLED	WORD	CLUE
EUAG	AGUE	A recurrent chill or fit of shivering
CIDYLPAL	PLACIDLY	Outwardly calm or composed; complacent
RINOACDS	SARDONIC	Mocking; cynical
SDEODTRCINCE	DISCONCERTED	Lacking self-composure
AELBDIRFMO	FORMIDABLE	Arousing fear or dread; awesome; difficult to overtake
EATBJC	ABJECT	Wretched; of the most contemptible kind
GBGELAEDDR	BEDRAGGLED	Made wet and limp
TXRIOPMYI	PROXIMITY	Closeness
SOMUNOI	OMINOUS	Portentous; foreboding
LPEIDIADADT	DILAPIDATED	Broken down; falling apart; ruined
TEEDDON	DENOTED	Marked; indicated; signified
REOMOS	MOROSE	Melancholy; gloomy; ill-humored
RIEAENOSAXPT	EXASPERATION	The state of extremely annoyed or irritated
DNAIIGNNLYT	INDIGNANTLY	With an anger aroused by something unjust
NCMEAGIN	MENACING	Threatening
SORB	ORBS	Eyes
ANNOIITCIDV	VINDICATION	The evidence or argument that justifies an act
EINDUIOCNATN	DENUNCIATION	An open condemnation or censure
SRDDIEENC	DISCERNED	Detected; perceived
LPYEUAERTLP	PERPETUALLY	Continually
OFROPER	REPROOF	Reprimand
DSAELUTSN	DAUNTLESS	Fearless; bold
TRRYPUNCEFO	PERFUNCTORY	Acting with little interest or care
CASIOAUUD	AUDACIOUS	Arrogantly insolent
IHTLEB	BLITHE	Cheerful; casual; carefree
ITOLANE	ELATION	Exalted feeling arising from a sense of triumph, power or relief
BDGOILE	OBLIGED	Caused to do something
ERESCTP	SPECTER	Ghost; phantasm
LMEABRNTNIIE	INTERMINABLE	Endless
OPUSDRGIOI	PRODIGIOUS	Enormous, extraordinary; marvelous
SUORDPNOE	PONDEROUS	Massive
NIDELNTHAIA	ANNIHILATED	Wiped out; destroyed completely
YCTUOIBSR	OBSCURITY	The condition of being unknown
EPSERO	REPOSE	Rest
OOTNTOICSRN	CONTORTIONS	Characterized by being twisted or bent out of shape
ULSNLE	SULLEN	Morose, sulky
DRTEBUAO	OBDURATE	Intractable; not giving

www.ingramcontent.com/pod-product-compliance
Lightning Source LLC
Chambersburg PA
CBHW051415070526
44584CB00023B/3446